# The Effective Constructivist Leader

## A Guide to the Successful Approaches

Arthur Shapiro

Rowman & Littlefield Education
Lanham • New York • Toronto • Plymouth, UK

Published in the United States of America
by Rowman & Littlefield Education
A division of Rowman & Littlefield Publishers, Inc.
A wholly owned subsidiary of The Rowman & Littlefield Publishing Group, Inc.
4501 Forbes Boulevard, Suite 200, Lanham, Maryland 20706
www.rowmaneducation.com

Estover Road, Plymouth PL6 7PY, United Kingdom

British Library Cataloguing in Publication Information Available

**Library of Congress Cataloging-in-Publication Data**

Shapiro, Arthur S.
  The effective constructivist leader : a guide to the successful approaches /
Arthur Shapiro.
    p.   cm.
  Includes bibliographical references.
  ISBN-13: 978-1-57886-727-1 (cloth : alk. paper)
  ISBN-10: 1-57886-727-4 (cloth : alk. paper)
  ISBN-13: 978-1-57886-728-8 (pbk. : alk. paper)
  ISBN-10: 1-57886-728-2 (pbk. : alk. paper)
  1. Constructivism (Education) 2. Teaching. 3. Educational leadership.
4. Constructivism (Education)—Case studies I. Title.
  LB1590.3.S4173 2008
  371.39—dc22

                                                          2007044920

I dedicate this book to my talented family: my wife, Sue Shapiro; my daughter, Alana Michelle Shapiro Thompson; my son, Dr. Marc Douglas Shapiro; my brother, Dr. Norman Shapiro; and my sister, Madeline Linick, all of whom had a strong hand in "constructing" me and my thinking. John Donne said, "No man is an island," and that is certainly true of me— and of all of us.

My gifted therapist-wife's strength in making it through a bout of breast cancer while remaining upbeat is one of her core attributes that I value so highly. And she is my partner, editor, and companion in our adventure. She urged me to write solo. You cannot ask for anything more. Our talented and loving daughter, who has persevered for two decades and is now entering the career of college teacher at the age of forty, continues to amaze me and others with her multidimensional abilities. Our brilliant, caring, creative, world-traveling son's persistence, determination, and focus pays off in unexpected ways as he moves through his career in political science and policy. My brilliant, multifaceted brother, Norman, can always be counted on to be supportive and to provide thoughtful insights. My talented, loving, and upbeat sister, Madeline, is always supportive.

Someone once said, "Lucky is the man whose family loves and supports him."

I am that man.

Thank you.

It is because modern education is so seldom inspired by a great hope that it so seldom achieves great results.

—Bertrand Russell, *Why Men Fight*

# Contents

# Acknowledgments

As I thought of the people who were indispensable in writing this book, several people readily came to mind. The first is my partner and wife, Sue, who urged me to write solo, who analyzed the ideas and their development, and edited with such clarity and insight. Friend and colleague Dr. Leanna Isaacson, who partnered in moving her very large elementary school into a constructivist model, with such impressive long-lasting outcomes, provided major grist for the mills of our thinking.

Lynne Menard, longtime friend and our department's Berbecker Fellow, edited, suggested, and immersed herself so that we could pull this off. Berbecker Fellow, computer guru, and friend Saundra Hart's energy and commitment finished the manuscript when it needed her expertise and thoughtful analysis. Jennifer Vincent, in her calm, expert way, made sure that all the figures and tables were computerized. Without her skill and timely help, this project could not be finished. My appreciation and thanks for the extraordinary insight and skill Andrea Mowatt and Amelia Van Name displayed in developing "The Constructivist Leader's Mental Checklist." The instrument richly portrays how to pull off a constructivist class. Jeff Hall's willingness to use his computer expertise was helpful in tight spots, as well.

To you, I give my thanks. Colleagues and friends are necessary.

# Prologue

## How Can This Book Help Me Become
## a Much Better Leader?

I hold that man is in the right who is most closely in league with the
future.

— Henrik Ibsen

It's been virtually three long decades since anyone has come up with a
new and exciting way of thinking about and practicing leadership. Leadership, obviously, has been a highly sexy topic for us Westerners since at
least Homer's time 3,200 years ago. Actually, we have been riveted by
leadership for all that time, in many cases worshipping it, certainly hon-
oring it. It's about time that we developed a new way of looking at and
pulling off effective leadership approaches. This book does that.

Actually, the way was paved in the middle of the last decade by the
work of Linda Lambert in developing insights into constructivist leadership, who pioneered the way for developing practical approaches to improve our professional leadership practice. This book, hopefully, extends
those beginning insights into a coherent, comprehensive approach so that
those of us who see ourselves as leaders, who like to be on the forefront,
who are action-oriented, who want to make a difference, can use the examples, the strategies, to move into effective constructivist leadership
practices. The best way to do this is to provide key practical tools and
strategies essential to pulling off effective leadership approaches.

Most of us think of tools as physical objects; however, ideas and concepts can be exceedingly useful tools. Think of a carpenter. He/she needs
good tools with which to produce quality work. To do this, he/she needs
to have a clear mental picture, a clear vision regarding what quality work

actually looks like *before* he/she starts a project—or he/she simply will be unable to create it.

If we were physicians, we would need both physical and mental tools to operate at the highest professional levels. The physical tools we see easily (stethoscope thrown carelessly over the neck, X-ray), but our mental tools are more important. In education, as in medicine, we need to be able to access our kit of diagnostic approaches, to dig back into our educational backgrounds to bring to bear the various potential diagnoses that can describe and analyze the symptoms we are uncovering, and then develop antidotes (read, change strategies) to correct the concerns and issues we face.

In short, mental models are absolutely essential tools to develop quality professional functioning. If we do not have those tools, how can we do anything but merely tinker at the edges of our looming challenges? Any practicing leader wanting to become increasingly effective must have a mental arsenal of models, a slew of conceptual arrows in his/her quiver, to cope successfully with the challenges we face. But, it is not nearly enough to cope. We must not have only the usual tools, but also key mental tools, conceptual models, clear-cut strategies to improve our professional leadership practices. That is exactly what this book does. It provides a range of clear models, key ideas, major strategies to improve our professional leadership.

Next, one of the most fundamental movements in education in the past several years has been first the emergence of constructivist teaching and next constructivist leadership practices and strategies. Of course, some of these have been around, but only recently have we begun to develop more of these as mental models and to recognize their value in improving our professional practice. And, only very recently have we begun to apply such practices to our leadership skills and mental models.

That's what this book is all about—it focuses on laying out practical constructivist tools, models, and strategies any leader must have in his/her armamentarium to become more successful, to meet the looming challenges zooming into our organizations.

# SO, WHAT'S CONSTRUCTIVIST TEACHING ALL ABOUT?

The overwhelming consensus as the twentieth century closed has been that knowledge is constructed.

—D. C. Phillips, *Constructivism in Education*

## Chapter One

# How Can I Recognize Constructivist Teaching in Teachers' Professional Practice?

## Two Case Studies

Constructivism has become the reigning paradigm in teacher education in America today.

—S. Hausfather, *Educational Horizons*

Change is the primary social fact, as surely as motion is the primary physical fact.

—John Dewey, *International Journal of Ethics*

### A COMMON SENSE WAY OF EXPLAINING THE IDEA

*Reflective Questions*

1. *What do we mean by constructivism?*
2. *What do teachers using constructivist practices do? How do they make it work?*

Whenever I mention the word **constructivism**, many teachers, administrators, laymen often ask, "Tell me what you mean by it." Here goes.

Although this may sound a bit strange, every one of us *constructs* the way we look at things, that is, our own world. But, let's take a look at how we actually build our world. Even if we're a twin, is the way we look at things the same as our twin's perceptions? Obviously not. If we have a brother or sister, do all of us see things the same way, have we developed the same perceptions of our family, people, money, art, school, work, sports, recreation?

When my brother and I once described our mother, my wife exclaimed, "You're describing two entirely different women!"

As we grow we all develop different experiences, which affect our attitudes, values, beliefs, perceptions, the different ways we look at things. Age, gender, and socioeconomic differences, as well as rural, urban, and suburban upbringings, and cultural differences, all provide different experiences. All these lead us to develop different perceptions, values, beliefs, attitudes, meanings we attach to different things that may be important to some of us, but not to others. Obviously, we can't have the same experiences.

Simply stated, constructivism means that each of us through our experiences builds different ways of looking at things, which cause us to develop different perceptions, even of the same things. It's easy to illustrate this. Just reflect on how different people describe an accident. Perceptions certainly vary, as different eyewitness descriptions of the same event prove.

One of the first to express this was Piaget, who as early as 1954 wrote a book with a stopper title, *The Construction of Reality in the Child*. He developed this insight in trying to figure out how children build their understandings, *their* insights into how things work in *their* world. And they do build them differently than we expect, sometimes startlingly differently, based upon their previous knowledge and experience. Simply, constructivism involves people constructing meaning based on their previous experiences and knowledge.

A simple example might help. My wife is an older twin. She spots twins way before I am aware of them, because they're much more significant to her. She, as the older, almost invariably can predict from a pair of twins' (even very young) behavior, who is the older. Her younger twin never thinks about that, and, as a result, birth order of twins is inconsequential to her.

Another simple-appearing example: My wife was brought up in the forests and mountains of Oregon. As a direct result, she is extremely alert to smoke in the distance, whereas I, brought up in Chicago, am fairly unaware of smoke until it is pretty heavy and/or fairly close. Depending on one's experience, and/or on one's location, fire in the forest is not a ho-hum matter.

The upshot of this is that through a variety of experiences, such as depending on where we live, our families, our location, the subculture we grow up in, and a host of other factors referred to above, each of us constructs our own different world of perceptions, beliefs, attitudes, and values than even the closest members in our families.

Constructivist thinking came alive for me when I saw Berger and Luck-mann's title *The Social Construction of Reality*, written in 1966. It absolutely stopped me dead in my tracks. The implications of this title, written by two reputable sociologists, were astounding! We—each of us—*construct our own reality*. The reflections above obviously support this.

It is normal for a book that has some academic pretensions (fortunately, this book doesn't have many) to look for support in literature. Philosopher D. C. Phillips was asked by the National Society for the Study of Education (NSSE) to edit a book on constructivism in education. Focusing on the nature of constructivism, Phillips stated,

> [T]his . . . type of constructivist view is that learners actively construct their own ("internal," as some would say) sets of meaning or understandings; knowledge is not a mere *copy* of the external world, nor is knowledge acquired by passive absorption or by simple transference from one person (a teacher) to another (a learner or knower). In sum, knowledge is *made*, not *acquired*. (2000, 7)

## A Little Summary, So Far

We've pretty clearly established that we construct our own perceptual (and even our conceptual) worlds. Time to move on to the subject of this chapter, that is, what does constructivist teaching look like and how can we recognize it when we bump into it—and even pull it off ourselves.

## WHAT DOES CONSTRUCTIVIST TEACHING LOOK LIKE? TWO CASE STUDIES

The best way to attack this is to provide a couple of very short case studies. So, here goes. We'll start first with a traditional classroom approach, then present a constructivist model, and have fun comparing and contrasting them.

## Case Study I: Classical/Traditional Approach

Claudia Geocaris (1996/1997), a science teacher, provided an insightful description of her former approach to teaching her subject to ninth graders. Thoughtfully—and mercifully—she indicated that she had abandoned this approach. Please note that the structure as well as processes she established caused her a good deal of discomfort, which led her to abandon them. Also, note who made *all* decisions and how involved students became—or didn't—because of her former needs to control.

> In the past years I took a traditional approach with a complex, but vitally important scientific concept. What is DNA and how does it contribute to genetics and the diversity of life? I usually presented material to students through lectures and labs. I explained key scientific discoveries and told students about the theories that resulted from the research. After presenting the material, I expected students to understand the relationships among DNA, RNA, proteins, and genetics. Although many students did, others did not; moreover, my students did not exhibit high levels of student engagement. (1996/1997, 72)

The students lack interest and involvement! No surprise!

## Case Study II: What Constructivist Teaching Looks Like

Sue Sharp left her middle school team meeting, charged into the classroom, and snatched a transparency for the overhead. Immediately, she wrote the day's agenda in her neat left-handed style:

State on your **post-meeting reaction (PMR) form** your long-term goals and today's objectives
Schedule for groups:
The Warriors: Greek armor, weapons, war strategies
The Tradesmen: Economic life: role of trade, agriculture, diet
The Politicians: Political arrangements: who made decisions, how made
The Fashioneers: Roles of genders, dress, responsibilities
The Artists: drama, comedy, architecture, arts, sculpture
Review of today's work
Planning, objectives for tomorrow
Materials, other resources needed
Wrap-up, assessment on the Group Planning or PMR form.

See figure 1.1 for this self- and group assessment form that structures the group's unit goals, daily objectives, and resources needed for the day.

A. Date: _____
B. Class: _____

C. Name of group: _____
D. Recorder: _____
E. Long-range goals:
   1) _____
   2) _____
   3) _____
F. Task(s) for today:
   1) _____
   2) _____
   3) _____
G. Amount accomplished (circle):

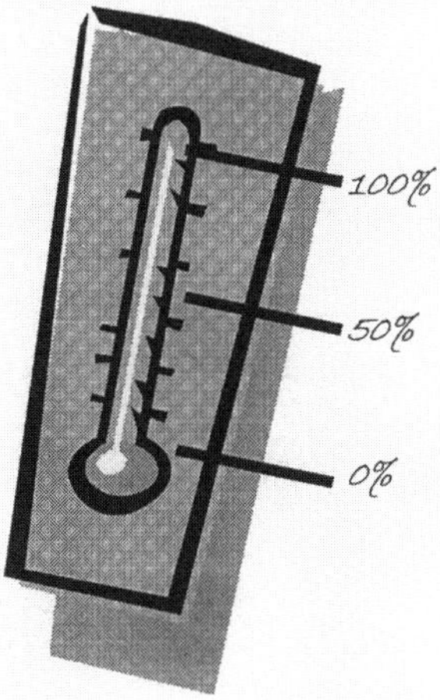

H. What helped you?
_____
_____
_____
_____
_____

I. What blocked you?
_____
_____
_____
_____
_____

J. Task(s) for tomorrow:
_____
_____

K. What resources do you need for tomorrow?:
   Human: _____
   Material: _____

**Figure 1.1.   Post-meeting Reaction (PMR) Form**

As the eighth graders surged into the room, she asked members from each group if they wanted to change any of yesterday's plans. The Tradesmen needed to send a couple of kids to the library to check out Greek home construction technology, so they needed passes.

As they came in, they immediately went over to their group areas and got to work. Sue sat with each group in turn, listening to their planning. All groups were working with lots of energy and interest. She sat and observed as the group working on Greek economic life made careful plans for a meal for the class. They asked if they could invite the principal, an assistant superintendent, the superintendent herself, and a board member. Ms. Sharp asked kids to think about putting "their best personal work" (Isaacson 2004) on the final PMR (handed out daily as a planning and assessment form) for the unit.

## TIME FOR ANALYSIS: COMPARE AND CONTRAST

*Reflective Question*

*Can you think of at least four major advantages of using constructivist practices in your teaching techniques?*

- Passive vs. active learner—which model structures student roles to be active or passive?
- Ms. Geocaris treats her kids as *individuals*. Ms. Sharp treats kids as members of **social systems**, that is, she structures kids into working in *groups*.
- Motivation: Ms. Sharp uses **Maslow's hierarchy of human needs** (1954) to meet her students' needs. Ms. Geocaris's model makes her seem unaware of students' needs and interests. Ms. Sharp meets each need level (safety, social, esteem, self-actualization).
- Ms. Sharp actively develops *relationships, connections* with her kids.
- Which model emphasizes higher-order thinking, solving problems, active decision making, reflection? Actually, in traditional classes, kids do have one of three decisions to make: Go along with the teacher, pay little or no attention, sabotage.
- How about trust? Who trusts students more?
- Which approach focuses on inquiry; which on experiential learning?

- Which group is learning to plan?
- How is each classroom organized? Rows vs. small group seating arrangements? Which facilitates communication?
- Do students have a voice in what they study? Do they have opportunity to make choices?
- Which model can provide experiences for different learning styles?
- Who is astute enough to *create* the classroom culture and climate?
- Which model *creates relationships* so kids can learn from teachers? Each other?
- How does Ms. Geocaris's control needs drive her teaching model?
- Which model is more successful in motivating kids?
- Which model leads to developing talents, leadership, taking initiatives, and decision-making skills more effectively?
- Which model values students' viewpoints?
- Which is perceived as more relevant by students?
- Which integrates assessment within the context of daily classroom interactions?
- In which do learners have final responsibility for their learning?
- Which approach develops a **community of learners**, which facilitates establishing positive relationships?
- Who begins to own the purpose and/or problem being worked on?

There's simply no comparison about the effectiveness of the two.

## KEY ELEMENTS IN CONSTRUCTIVIST TEACHING

When we walk into a restaurant, how can we tell if it is a good one? Are waiters or waitresses well dressed? Are tables draped with tablecloths? Cloth napkins? Is there a sense of dignity? What do menus look like? Prices? (They can give us a clue.)

*Reflective Question*

*What elements tell you very quickly if you have a constructivist classroom?*

- Are kids in rows? Looking bored? Forget it.
- Are they in groups? Are groups the basic vehicle for instruction? A good sign.
- What size are groups? No less than four, no more than seven (Thelen 1949), although if collaborative learning is the model, groups of two often are used.
- Do kids follow ground rules (into which they've had input) to make groups effective?

  —listen to others

  —politely accept divergent viewpoints

  —never put anyone or any idea down (which generates a feeling of safety)
- Is the class interactive (that is, are they working with each other)?
- Is active learning going on? That is, are kids involved in doing things, often in groups (since much learning occurs in social situations for most people? Even reflection is social in nature, since we are having a conversation with ourselves.)
- Who generates curriculum? Are kids involved? If so, it is an **emergent curriculum**.
- Do kids feel safe, respected, not attacked, picked on?
- Are social and esteem needs being met and are a variety of roles created (recorder, reporter, concern for meeting time and task requirements, concern for people's and groups' feelings)?
- Are kids taking responsibility, enjoying themselves (which means a good deal of noise sometimes)?
- Do we see kids' creativity encouraged?
- Which environment tends to provide more support so that people will take more risks without fear?
- Which provides a framework for relationships, community, team, and trust building, that is, facilitates building a community of learners?
- Which approach seems to stimulate critical thinking more?

## SUMMARY

Hopefully, we've laid out key elements of a constructivist approach to teaching. Next, while this is a primer, we still need a bit more depth in describing and analyzing what constructivist teaching looks like. Chapter 2 plunges more deeply into practical insights for how to pull off constructivist teaching and leadership with an organized checklist developed by two psychologists in my classes, which they called the Constructivist Leader's Mental Checklist. The last chunk of chapter 2 provides a brief flyover of the range of constructivist schools of thought.

## GLOSSARY

**community of learners**   treating a class as a group with common purposes, rather than a bunch of unrelated individuals who happen to be in the same room.

**constructivism**   a view of learning that each individual actively constructs his/her meanings and understandings. Knowledge is made, not acquired.

**emergent curriculum**   a curriculum generated from students' needs and interests.

**Maslow's hierarchy of human needs**   see next chapter.

**post-meeting reaction (PMR) form**   a group planning form which structures out the group's goals, daily objectives, and resources needed.

**social system**   the basic human unit is the small group—any two or more people in a meaningful relationship.

## Chapter Two

# How to Think Like a Constructivist Teacher and Leader in Designing Your Classroom and Team

The people who get on in this world are the people who get up and look for the circumstances they want, and if they can't find them, make them.

—George Bernard Shaw

All things are created twice. First, mentally, and then physically. Building a house is the best example. It is created in every detail before the ground is even touched. When the physical creation begins, every decision is governed by the first (mental) creation.

—Stephen Corey

As promised in the summary of chapter 1, first we'll provide key elements in building a constructivist classroom or team, followed by a detailed checklist, "The **Constructivist Leader's Mental Checklist**," by Andrea Mowatt and Amelia Van Name (2002), two psychologists who were challenged by pulling off a constructivist classroom. Additionally, they focused on processes and structures anyone in a leadership position who wants to move into constructivist leadership practices might use in that process. The third and (mercifully) brief section is a sortie into major forms of constructivist thinking.

## KEY DESIGN ELEMENTS

*Reflective Question*

*If you were to design a checklist focusing on key elements in constructivist teaching and leadership, what would you pick to emphasize?*

# MOTIVATION: AN INTRODUCTION—MASLOW
# (VERY BRIEFLY)

## Physiological Needs

We can choose a number of different explanations for the way we behave, such as **Maslow's hierarchy of human needs** (1954), which also
provides useful insights into creating successful cultures for constructivist (or, any) classrooms. He believed that the first level we must satisfy consists of our physiological needs (food, air, water, shelter, and
[fortunately], sex). Schools meet food needs with breakfast for kids
needing it and lunch for all. A lot of sharp teachers generate parties using food, such as pizza and ice cream, as rewards and recognition, popular with kids as well as adults. Implications for school leaders relate
to the district's capacity to establish salary schedules to satisfy those
needs.

## Safety Needs

Maslow's second level comprises our safety needs, consisting of physical
and emotional safety, which can only be met if our physiological needs
have been satisfied. Safety needs can be a bit tricky in schools, because
kids and adults have to feel they're not going to be attacked physically or
emotionally in hallways, bathrooms, and classes. This means that we do
not like being ridiculed, targeted, or bullied by our peers, nor by teachers,
principals, or leaders. The example of Columbine High School has become seared into our American consciousness. Recently, schools have
been implementing antibullying initiatives.

If classrooms are safe, people can feel free to express themselves and
their viewpoints, be creative, even reveal personal feelings and matters. If
not, we are careful and we watch ourselves. We may even shut down. The
classroom loses its potential for dynamism, excitement. What else can you
think of to stimulate safety?

This clearly implies that we educators have to look inward to see if we
ourselves pick on kids in classrooms or colleagues. If so, how can they or
anyone else feel safe? Safety in schools and classrooms is a goal to be
achieved by faculty and leaders agreeing that there will be no personal

criticism, that the norm of acceptance of others' ideas is to be respected. Respect is essential to satisfy this need. And, treating everything said as confidential ensures freedom for expressing viewpoints.

*Reflective Questions*

1. *What can leaders do to make sure that we feel safe in our schools?*
2. *What can you do? (One norm we can develop is that everything said here stays here.)*
3. *How about our own personal spaces, such as in our families?*

## Social Needs

Once the preceding two levels have been met, according to Maslow, social needs of acceptance, love, and belonging are next. After all, we humans are social beings. How does this play out? We spend large amounts of our waking time in classrooms and schools, which are social systems (that is, two or more people in meaningful interaction), and where much satisfaction or dissatisfaction in our working lives can occur. Since most of us seem to need approval by others and seem to want to socialize, school settings can be organized to generate great satisfaction.

How to pull this off? If we want to meet social and psychological needs as well as academic needs, using small groups is a natural, particularly in light of Kurt Lewin's (1952a) findings that if we want to be effective in changing attitudes and behavior, making such changes *in public in small groups* is key. People who promise they will do something publicly in a small group are much more likely to carry out their commitments. This contrasts with *individuals* urged to change behavior in classrooms or lectures—who generally don't.

The small group meets basic social needs if it is healthy and does not support excessively critical or antisocial behavior. Their value for effective instruction is that people tend to bond with each other, thus building emotional ties and therefore supportive behavior. A movement in education consists of developing *communities of learners and professional learning communities* for faculty and leadership.

*Reflective Questions*

*1. Can you think of people whose social needs have not been met?*
*2. How hungry do they appear for approval, a level on which they are stuck and struggle daily?*

Do you recall a president of the United States who always saw himself as an outsider, which led him to imagine that he had a long list of enemies? It did not serve him well.

Do our schools provide for meeting leaders', teachers', and kids' social needs? How can this be improved? Would decentralizing into smaller units facilitate this? It does exactly that, but we keep building bigger and bigger schools thinking that they will be more economical. They aren't, even if we do not count the social costs of excessive size, such as dropouts, etc., so, we have to develop small learning communities (SLCs) to undo negatives of large size.

*Reflective Questions*

*1. Do your middle and high schools have central areas where kids can mill around and relate to each other?*
*2. How else can we organize our classes and schools so that children and faculty can satisfy their social needs?*

Decentralizing certainly is one key. The Gregorc Personality Style Delineator, an instrument discussed in chapter 3, can be of considerable assistance in developing grouping models for classrooms—and for faculties and administrative teams.

## Esteem Needs

Maslow's fourth level consists of getting prestige, respect, and recognition from others, involving our self-esteem. A vehicle for this is that no destructive criticism is to occur, everyone's contribution is valued, respect is given to everyone.

My son, when he was about nine years old, palled around with some very sharp kids. One boy hung on the periphery wanting very much to join. The boys decided that he needed recognition badly (I picked this up when I overheard them discussing it). Note that nine-year-olds intuitively figured out social and esteem needs.

## Reflective Question

*What can we do to increase the esteem of kids, faculty, and people in leadership positions?*

Decentralizing schools into smaller units ensures that we know each other and so can communicate and socialize more readily, discussed in chapter 11. Similarly, the suggestion to decentralize classes by using small groups as the basic vehicle does the same thing.

What else can we do to make sure that people respect each other and recognize accomplishments? One technique I've recommended is to establish a Recognition Committee. Usually they place photos of *everyone* who has done something that should receive recognition, with a statement about what he/she did, in a heavily trafficked area (often by the administrative offices). So, taking Maslow seriously pays dividends.

## Aesthetic Needs

Recent reexamination of Maslow's work by Maslow and Stephens (2000) leads them to conclude that we have a need for aesthetics expressed in various forms of art and artistic expression. They noted:

> If we have clearly in mind the educational goals for human beings that I will be hinting at, if we hope for our children that they will become full human beings, and that they will move toward actualizing the potentialities that they have, then, as nearly as I can make out, the only kind of education in existence today that has any faint inkling of such goals is art education. (2000, 187–88)

Maslow further supported this by developing "18 Moments of Creativeness," including concepts of "Fullest Spontaneity," "Fullest Expressiveness" (of uniqueness), and "Acceptance."

## Self-Actualized Needs

Maslow's last level consists of becoming self-actualized, developing into what we are capable of becoming, being self-directed, autonomous. He portrayed this as rare, citing those at the top of their game, such as Eleanor Roosevelt and Mahatma Gandhi, who had met their preceding "lower" needs. Mrs. Roosevelt, ambassador to the United Nations, would take the subway, not needing to impress others by making a grand entrance from a limousine. Self-actualization, then, describes people who seem to feel that they've "arrived," who do not need to impress others, who are happy and satisfied with their lives, with their achievements.

As I write this, I realize that my father had reached that state for the last couple of decades of his life. He felt that he was a highly successful father and person, since he believed that his two sons and daughter had achieved success.

*Reflective Questions*

1. *Whom do you know who feels he/she has achieved such a level? Paul Newman? General Schwarzkopf?*
2. *Do you know of any politician? George Washington? Thomas Jefferson?*
3. *Do you know anyone in a leadership position in our schools operating on this level?*

Even more interesting questions are how can we in leadership positions facilitate colleagues and students in reaching this level? How can leaders themselves organize to move to this level in their schools (and other organizations)? It certainly is a worthwhile goal for a constructivist social system. Hopefully, we can help you achieve this.

## Other Motivational Practices

Using Great Books questions to analyze articles and readings can be useful. Three questions usually are:

1. What does the author say? What are the major points, assumptions, beliefs?

2. Are they valid?
3. How can I/we use them today?

I use chart paper with small groups since that involves everyone. Roles can then be multiplied, with recorders being different than reporters. Note the motivation by participating in small groups. Students tend to do assigned readings, particularly if instructors are wise enough in setting norms that it is an expectation, *a social compact*, that everyone reads assignments. Students do not like looks they get from their peers if they fail to uphold their end of the bargain.

Since each group works independently, putting chart paper on the board tends to be a motivator to think thoroughly, since everyone compares his/her own product with other groups, an interesting process to watch (and to cue kids into watching themselves).

## INSTRUCTIONAL DELIVERY SYSTEMS/VEHICLES

The classroom is designed to be constructivist, interactive, and experiential, certainly with a good deal of active learning, and with time built in for reflection (a disappearing commodity with our testing mania today). The theoretical basis lies in classical works in education, social psychology, and group dynamics, as well as anthropology, including Dewey (1938), Lewin (1952a), Piaget (1954), Thelen (1949), Mead (1934), Berger and Luckmann (1966), Brooks and Brooks (1993), Linton (1955), and Goffman (1967). In curriculum, Bloom (1956), Goodlad (1984), Tyler (1949), and Benjamin (1939) are sources.

## CREATING A CULTURE YOU LIKE

*Reflective Questions*

1. *How did you create the culture in your family? That is, what norms/ customs did you deliberately choose?*
2. *How about in your class or school, team or department?*

Most of us create a culture in our organizations without knowing that we are doing exactly that. Then, if destructive customs get in the way, we are irritated with students. But, if we're astute enough to create our own, we can avoid such situations. The paragraphs above provide clear ideas about how to go about creating positive cultures. For example, following Maslow, if we make sure the classroom is safe, people can become more creative, free, supportive.

## Size of the Small Group

Thelen (1949) studied how small group size makes for success, concluding that to generate ideas, the minimum number had to be no less than four. If the group exceeded seven, a more aggressive person would squeeze out a less aggressive individual, since we could not develop more than seven roles. With small size, groups usually become sounding boards and support groups to improve our ideas and products.

## Active Learning

Davis and Murrell (1993) wrote, "What the research on student learning has concluded is that the more actively students are involved in the learning process and take personal responsibility for their learning outcomes, the greater are the learning results." If we take this seriously, we have to make sure that students are actively involved. If not, learning is reduced. Marlowe and Page (1998) noted, "The research as a whole shows active learning methods to be superior to teacher-dominated approaches in measures of academic, affective, and skill learning" (19).

## AN EMERGENT CURRICULUM—AND TODAY, I LEARNED ... AND MY MOST SIGNIFICANT LEARNINGS ...

While the testing mania is distorting education, whenever I ask students what they want to learn, they inevitably cite the very goals I think useful—and, often some I've not thought of. Bloom's taxonomy (1956) is a vital element in creating a constructivist environment. At the end of every session, we use a sentence stem, "Today, I learned ... ," which encourages students to reflect. Responses are usually quite insightful and thoughtful. At the middle and end of the semester, we ask for student's "Most Significant

Learnings," which often become major productions, planned for weeks. In short, we make a social compact.

The following table represents two students' joint effort analyzing and synthesizing their "Most Significant Learnings in this Class."

**Table 2.1.   Constructivist Leader's Mental Checklist**

*The following sections have been designed to assess one's readiness to participate in a group as a constructivist leader. The checklist was developed to assist the constructivist leader in answering the question, "Am I ready to facilitate group process?"*

**Component 1: Personal Readiness of the Facilitator**
1. I have developed an understanding of my personality characteristics as well as my typical interaction or communication style in groups.
2. I have developed an understanding of others' personalities and communication skills.
3. I accept and respect other personality styles.
4. I understand how to communicate with a variety of personality styles.
5. I am prepared to set the tone for effective group process by taking on the role of a facilitator, even if my tendency is to teach or lead in a role other than that of facilitator (e.g., more directive).
6. I understand that I must maintain an ongoing awareness of my own beliefs and values and use this self-awareness to promote an environment conducive to learning, both for individuals with similar beliefs and values as well as those with differing beliefs and values.
7. I understand my own learning style as well as other learning styles.
8. I understand and am prepared to teach people with different learning styles, including my own.
9. I am prepared to model the essential underpinning of Constructivist Leadership.
10. I am prepared to observe group process closely and to make decisions based on my observations to facilitate optimal group functioning.

**Component 2: Structuring the Environment**
1. The room design is such that it facilitates structuring for group process (adequate lighting ability to control temperature, flexibility to arrange room, can accommodate workgroups).
2. There are enough tables and chairs to arrange participants into small workgroups (maximum of seven members per group).
3. Chairs are strategically placed near the various workgroups to allow the facilitator easy access to individual groups.
4. An area is made available for the presentation of food and beverages.
5. 24" × 36" newsprint and writing implements are available.
6. There are plenty of name tags or name cards.
7. Relevant, interest-driven reading materials have been copied for distribution.

**Component 3: Setting the Tone**
1. **Creating a safe learning environment:**
   - Group members are asked to learn about a person in close proximity
   - Ample time afforded for introductions (introduction of another group and self-introductions) during first two meetings

*(continued)*

**Table 2.1.** (*continued*)

---

- Confidentiality is established (members are asked to agree that "it is safe to speak in a group" because "what is said in the group stays in the group")
- The facilitator encourages and supports risk-taking and sharing of personal information
- The facilitator makes it known that "all contributions will be valued"
- The facilitator models acceptance, respect, and validation of individuals and varying viewpoints
- Although high expectations and a sense of personal responsibility are clearly communicated, anxiety is reduced through acceptance of situations impeding group attendance and timely arrival to group
- Through a collaborative discussion of evaluation methods and ownership for learning, the learning environment becomes less threatening
- Refreshment breaks allow for informal sharing of information, development of more intimate relationships, and the establishment of a safe community

2. **Addressing social needs:**
   - Participants are arranged in small workgroups
   - Small and large group interaction/discussion is emphasized
   - A list of names, phone numbers, and addresses is compiled and distributed to group members to promote networking during and after-group sessions (the facilitator's information is included in the same format and is placed in alphabetical order, within the list of group members, to establish and promote balanced power)
   - It is made clear that refreshment breaks, in part, provide a more relaxed atmosphere for socialization and "bonding" of group members

3. **Fostering motivation (making it relevant):**
   - The facilitator asks key questions to promote input and shared decision making regarding arrival and dismissal time, assessment format, relevant content, and group goals
   - The facilitator accepts and manages student responses to develop a sense of ownership by group members
   - Individuals are asked to write their goals/objectives for the class
   - The facilitator indicates that all contributions are valuable and should not be dismissed
   - Groups are requested to compile the individual goals on newsprint
   - Group goals are posted, presented, discussed
   - The facilitator compares and contrasts goals and points out the similarities of groups as well as the diversity and creativity both within and across groups
   - Group goals are compiled and distributed at the next meeting
   - The compiled list of goals is used to develop a syllabus that best meets the unique needs and interests of the group
   - As group members raise questions, the questions are used to guide group discussion and when consistent with the goal of the group, are used to guide the selection of relevant reading materials
   - Group members are told that they are responsible for their learning
   - The routine participation in workgroups established the implicit norm for advanced preparation of the individual prior to meaningful engagement in group activities

- Individuals are given choices about the format and the content of the midterm and final and are told that they are responsible for demonstrating their "most significant learning in the class" either individually or with a group

4. **Satisfying esteem needs:**
   - Group members are given multiple opportunities to express ideas
   - The facilitator communicates that varying viewpoints are encouraged, accepted, and valued
   - Contributions are honored by connecting ideas shared in class with relevant content information
   - Sharing of ideas and relevant personal information is promoted by thanking individuals for sharing and by providing positive feedback when contributions are made
   - A constructive versus destructive criticism norm is encouraged, modeled, and reinforced
   - Formal recognition (positive feedback and applause) is provided for each small group contribution

5. **Meeting physiological needs:**
   - A refreshment break is scheduled
   - When possible, groups are scheduled at an optimal and convenient time for learning/working
   - Movement and group interaction are incorporated to reduce restlessness, inattention, and physical discomfort

## Component 4: Instructional Format

1. An agenda is posted each session and, at a minimum, includes information to be covered, group work time, group presentation and discussion, the refreshment break and the phrase, "Today I learned . . ."
2. Group-generated goals and areas of interest expressed by group members guide the topics selected for coverage in the group.
3. The facilitator selects readings relevant to the goal of the group and based on the interest expressed by group members.
4. Individuals are assigned tasks (e.g., reading) either in class or before class to prepare for group work.
5. Individuals are constantly encouraged to watch group dynamics, to relate observations to key concepts covered in the course, and to develop an awareness of the interrelationship between leadership and group behavior.
6. Individuals and groups engage in a variety of tasks to promote self-awareness.
7. The following questions (adapted from the Great Books program) are posted: What does the author state? What are the major points, assumptions, and beliefs? Are they valid? How can we utilize them today in our professional practice?
8. Individuals are arranged in small (no more than seven members) workgroups.
9. Workgroups discuss and organize responses to the posted questions.
10. Workgroups present their responses to the entire group.
11. Individuals then have the opportunity to comment on or question information presented by workgroups.
12. The facilitator interjects as necessary to make salient key points, to link newly introduced concepts to previously covered concepts, and to prime group members for future learning experiences.

*(continued)*

**Table 2.1.** (*continued*)

13. The facilitator consistently encourages and models acceptance of the contributions.
14. The facilitator acknowledges the difficult nature of sharing information and thanks individuals for sharing feedback, insight, and relevant personal experiences.
15. Group members are given ample time to eat and to engage in conversation during refreshment break.
16. Group members are invited to use the phrase, "Today, I learned . . ." to articulate a concept or insight they have gained from that particular group experience.
17. When applicable, the group is assigned a task to prepare for the next session.
18. **Understanding and application of theory, activities, and insights is facilitated by:**
    - Small and large group participation and discussion
    - Opportunities to share what has been learned using the sentence stem: "Today, I learned . . ."
    - Observation and discussion of group process
    - Observation and discussion of facilitator's actions and comments (modeling)
    - Tasks designed to increase self-awareness
    - Engagement in the midterm and final projects emphasizing one's "most significant learnings"

**Component 5: Monitoring Group Process (Watch & Listen)**
1. **Is the environment safe and relatively stress free?**
    - When asked about the norms of the group, do group members express that they feel comfortable discussing opinions, asking questions, sharing personal information and giving/receiving feedback?
    - Are group members demonstrating a sense of safety by revealing personal information, asking questions, taking risks, expressing opinions, and giving/receiving feedback?
2. **Are relationships developing?**
    - Do individuals appear to be engaged and interacting with one another in a comfortable manner during (small group) work sessions?
    - Do individuals appear to be engaged and interacting with one another in a comfortable manner during the refreshment break?
3. **Are individuals accepting responsibility for their learning?**
    - When asked about the norms of the group, do group members state that individuals are responsible for their own learning?
    - As the facilitator moves about the group, does it appear that group members are prepared and contributing to the group process?
    - If issues arise within the group, does the facilitator encourage self-correction among group members?
    - Are roles developing as indicated by the actions of the individuals within groups (e.g., engagement in discussion, rotation of responsibilities for writing, and presentation of ideas to the entire group)?
    - Do individuals ask and answer questions?
    - Do individuals produce a thoughtful midterm and final project reflecting active participation in the learning process?
4. **Are individuals and workgroups demonstrating knowledge as indicated by:**
    - Discussions in workgroups
    - Listening and participation in small and large groups
    - Observations of individuals and group dynamics

- Content of workgroup presentations
- Large group discussions
- Individual questions and comments
- Responses associated with the sentence stem of "Today, I learned . . ."
- Content of presentations of "most significant learning" projects

*Source:* Checklist developed by Andrea M. Mowatt, Ed.S. & Amelia D. Van Name, Ed.S. in the spring of 2002 as a midterm project for one of Dr. Shapiro's graduate-level leadership courses at the University of South Florida. The checklist reflects concepts published by Dr. Shapiro and addressed in the course.

## MAJOR FORMS OF CONSTRUCTIVISM

Philosopher D. C. Phillips (2000) was commissioned to write a book about constructivist thinking by the National Society for the Study of Education. He parsed out two major forms—**psychological** and **social constructivism**. I'll take a very brief stab at each with its consequences.

Phillips notes that psychological constructivism:

> refers to a set of views about how individuals learn (and about how those who help them to learn ought to teach). Roughly, this . . . type of constructivist view is that learners actively construct their own ("internal," as some would say) sets of meanings or understandings; knowledge is not a mere *copy* of the external world, nor is knowledge acquired by mere passive absorption or by simple transference from one person (a teacher) to another (a learner or knower). In sum, knowledge is *made*, not *acquired*. (7)

Why is this psychological constructivism? Phillips explains:

> Some constructivists of this broad type go on to stress that we cannot be certain any two individuals will construct the same understandings; even if they use the same linguistic formulations to express what they have learned, their deep understandings might be quite different. . . . In previous papers I have used the expression *psychological constructivism*, because the center of interest is the *psychological understandings of individual learners.* (7)

We discussed this in chapter 1.

Of course, academics always develop schools of thought and constructivist thought is not immune to this branching. The chief spokesman for a radical psychological constructivist school is Ernst von Glasersfeld, considered by Phillips a giant in the field. He states:

> Radical constructivism . . . starts from the assumption that knowledge, no matter how it is defined, is in the heads of persons, and that the thinking subject has no alternative but to construct what he or she knows on the basis of his or her own experience. What we can make of experience constitutes the only world we consciously live in. . . . All kinds of experience are essentially subjective, and though I may find reasons to believe that my experience may not be unlike yours, I have no way of knowing that it is the same. . . . Taken seriously, this is a profoundly shocking view. (1998, 1)

Von Glasersfeld is correct since he asserts that because you and I never fully share the same experiences, we can never perceive the same things similarly. We noted that in chapter 1, talking about twins. His view is radical, but he misses key processes that make us human, that make us become social animals, the great power of culture and its underpinning vehicle, language. Because of this we speak the same language, learn the same customs. George Herbert Mead (1934) pointed out that the human mind, the self we all form, and our society are all socially formed.

## Social Constructivism

This second form of constructivism is analyzed by Phillips:

> "Constructivism" embodies a thesis about the disciplines or bodies of knowledge that have been built up during the course of human history. I have described this thesis as, roughly, that these disciplines (or public bodies of knowledge) are human constructs, and that the form that knowledge has taken in these fields has been determined by such things as politics, ideologies, values, the exertion of power and preservation of status, religious beliefs, and economic self-interest. This thesis denies that the disciplines are objective reflections of an "external world." (2000, 6)

*Reflective Question*

*What does this mean? Is scientific knowledge socially constructed? Now that's a radical thought!*

As with psychological constructivism, we have moderate and radical social constructivism—with the latter erupting into the "science wars." First, we'll deal with moderate social constructivism and then the radical brand—you choose which you prefer.

Very briefly, moderate social constructivism believes that the *social world* is socially constructed, as Berger and Luckmann's title, *The Social Construction of Reality*, clearly implies. If we look at a high school, many of its rituals and customs have developed over the relatively short time of about 150 years. Early high schools did not have homecoming queens, football games (invented later), or bus schedules.

Radical social constructivists push the envelope rather hard. These sociologists, labeled "the Strong Program in the sociology of knowledge" believe

> that the form that knowledge takes in a discipline can be *fully explained*, or *entirely accounted for*, in sociological terms. That is, . . . what is taken to be knowledge in any field has been determined by sociological forces including the influence of ideologies, religion, human interests, group dynamics, and so forth . . . this group of thinkers wishes to deny that so-called knowledge is in any sense a reflection or copy of that "external reality" that the community in question is investigating. (Phillips 2000, 8–9)

Radical social constructivists state that even so-called hard sciences are socially constructed, so that they cannot claim objectivity, clearly difficult for hard scientists to swallow. In other words, this viewpoint claims that the structure and knowledge of the sciences and even mathematics are determined by social forces. They claim that the vaunted objectivity our culture accords to these fields is a delusion. If we take this seriously, how can we tell science from myth, from nonsense? If science and mathematics have no objectivity and validity, what does this do to our ideas about knowledge?

As you can imagine, many scientists have become apoplectic over this, which is why this is called the "science wars." But, wait—Phillips notes:

> The concepts we use in everyday life or in the scholarly disciplines, did not descend—fully formed—out of the blue. There was a time when the concepts of "energy" or "mass" or "molecule" or "psychosis" or "working class" did not exist; and the halting and interactive process can be traced

whereby these concepts and the very things or categories themselves were developed. (2000, 88)

**Critical constructivism** has been explored recently by Kinchloe (2005), and adds to our armamentarium of tools to analyze our constructed world. Major foci of this work include "exploring the complex relationship between teaching and learning and knowledge production and research" (3). Kinchloe directs a good deal of attention to the relationship between power and knowledge production in education.

## SUMMARY

Hopefully, this has been a brief excursion into key elements in designing and running a constructivist classroom/team starting with Maslow, creating instructional delivery systems, including a supportive culture, using small groups, with active learning, and reflection. Next, we presented the Constructivist Leader's Mental Checklist, and finished with a brief flyover of some major forms of constructivist thinking.

A word of caution: People who want to try this model often feel that they have to jump into it whole hog—probably not a good move. It's wise to try one element here, another there. But, for certain, it is absolutely crucial to set up ground rules for group work before starting, such as listening respectfully, not interrupting.

It is a good idea to ask kids to develop sensible ground rules first, and, afterward, ask them how they liked it, how it went. It's a good move to ask how to improve the process so ground rules can be altered. Kids have good common sense, and if they feel safe, can be quite objective, loving input into what goes on. Besides, in constructivism, their input is not only an essential component, it is invaluable (comprising a primary motivator)—and is necessary in developing a community of learners.

## GLOSSARY

**Constructivist Leader's Mental Checklist**   a checklist developed by two psychologists to describe a constructivist classroom and leader behavior.

**critical constructivism**   focuses on the impact of power and elites on the way we construct our knowledge.

**Maslow's hierarchy of human needs**   a system of analyzing human needs developed by psychologist Abraham Maslow.

**psychological constructivism**   focuses on how individuals learn.

**social constructivism**   a viewpoint focusing on the insight that the social world is socially constructed.

# TOOLS TO UNDERSTAND OURSELVES, OUR KIDS, OUR COWORKERS

The two indispensable prerequisites for successful leadership are that the leader know and understand himself, and know and understand the times in which he lives.

—Benjamin Disraeli, British prime minister

*Chapter Three*

# What Makes Terry Tick?

## Our Needs for Power, Control, Recognition, Safety, Acceptance, Esteem, and How Constructivism Helps Satisfy Them

There are utterly destructive consequences of acting *without knowing* what one is doing.

— Bruno Bettelheim, psychoanalyst

Personality, too, is destiny.

— Erik H. Erikson, *Newsweek*

Since we've constructed a genderless title, we can proceed hoping that no one will take offense—and, hopefully, in keeping with the purposes of this book, this information will be useful.

*Reflective Question*

*Why be concerned about what makes kids (and, all of us) tick?*

When I was a director of secondary education in the somewhat rural capital city of a small state, we had a national shortage of teachers. The solution? Try to hire some sharp liberal arts graduates. I did exactly that. We found a number of very able young liberal arts graduates—all winners I thought, and they came on board. The result? A disaster! The woman I thought was the best and brightest literally walked out before the first period of day one ended. I was astounded—it was tragic, but I learned. The rest? All had fatal—not major—*fatal* flaws. We asked, Why?

33

1. They did not understand kids, their behavior, or what motivated them.
2. They had no idea how kids learned.
3. Therefore, they did not know how to design lesson plans that worked.
4. They did not know what curriculum was, or how to build it.
5. They did not know how to work with kids, establish relationships with them, how to teach them.
6. Oddly, although they had lived in K–12 schools for at least a dozen or more years, they really did not know what made schools tick, how they worked.

Other than these deficits, they fared miserably. What they fell back on was their memories of what they saw modeled, which did not work. They simply were unprepared. Incidentally, we didn't throw them into the most difficult classes. Wisely, I gave up doing this. But, in this time of teacher shortages, we're repeating this pseudosolution.

Why am I describing this sad incident in this chapter? Simply, if we do not understand what makes kids (and all of us) behave, we cannot be effective in working with and relating to people. So, let us take a look at different ways of getting a handle on why we behave the way we do. In this chapter, we will work on some ideas regarding how and why individuals behave. First, we'll refer to *Maslow's insights*, next **Gregorc's very practical personality styles** approach to understanding ourselves and others, then **Kohlberg's stages of moral reasoning** (it sure helps to know in what stages of moral thinking our friends, colleagues, supervisors, kids, even family members operate). We deal with **Glasser's reality therapy** and **George Herbert Mead's symbolic interaction** approach, fundamental insights into how we humans develop. We briefly point to *Calvin Taylor's* fascinating idea that we possess many talents, making us above average in at least one or more talent, and, last, *Davis McClelland's achievement motivation* approach.

The first of two chapters on what makes organizations tick is chapter 4 (a quick guide to how organizations work), and then chapter 5, on hidden behavior, lays out the impact of organizations and their culture and social systems on our behavior. Hopefully, we will recognize how constructivist approaches serve to meet those needs head on, as implied in this chapter.

## MASLOW'S HIERARCHY OF NEEDS

We have discussed each level relatively thoroughly in chapter 2, so let's move on. Needless to say, his levels are useful in teaching, leadership, and any relationship we develop.

## POWER AND CONTROL

*Reflective Questions*

*1. Do we all need and want power and control to run our lives the way we would like to do so?*
*2. Do you?*

I certainly do.

As we will see in the next section on Gregorc's contribution toward understanding others and ourselves, a goodly number of people, particularly those with one personality style, are into power and control. We used to think that the source of having power came from those in higher levels of authority giving it to lower levels, but we now know that one's power comes from our subordinates *accepting* our power (Barnard 1938). (See chapters 4 and 8 on power and influence.) That involves our own children, too. If our subordinates and kids decide not to accept our power, we do not have it. Now, that's a fundamental statement that a lot of us have difficulty accepting. If our subordinates, or kids, decide not to listen to us — goodbye power. It has evaporated. And it's not coming back without a lot of pain and changing our behavior — if ever.

Oddly, we begin to realize that we can increase our power by giving it away, by involving people in decision making (a fundamental strategy of building constructivist social systems). This makes control unnecessary — we can focus on achieving goals, rather than on trying to control others, a losing strategy anyway.

Manipulative behavior is focused on controlling others, which is why the word itself has negative connotations. People with control needs often try to dominate their groups, their organizations. Have you ever watched two people (especially obvious in those who are married) butt heads over who is going to dominate? In one of my wife's classes, a woman with a high concrete sequential score (on Gregorc's delineator) phoned her husband during a break and asked him to describe her in a word. His response? Dominating.

A last comment on this brief section on power and control: Authoritarian use of power is the opposite of constructivism.


## GREGORC'S MIND STYLES DELINEATOR: INSIGHTS

Anthony Gregorc, formerly a teacher, high school principal, assistant superintendent, and last, a university professor, became aware of *patterns* of behavior he observed, and developed the *Gregorc Style Delineator* (1982b), explained more fully by the *Mind Styles Model: Theory, Principles and Practice* (1998/2004). He realized that people *perceived* the world generally in one of two patterns, usually *concretely* or, on the other hand, *abstractly*. Although most of us can do both, we tend to lean toward one or the other pattern. For example, people who perceive the world concretely like to deal with facts, details, actual physical things. At the other end of this continuum, those who tend to live more abstractly either express their emotions and feelings or live in the world of ideas and concepts.

He then saw patterns in how people *ordered* their world. Some ordered the way they functioned *sequentially*, doing one thing a time, usually in order, living in their world more linearly. Others operated more *randomly*, doing many things at a time, such as working on a lot of projects (often leaving some partly finished), reading several books at a time, not having much order in their lives. Figure 3.1 illustrates this model.

We have an instrument providing four styles, which at higher scores tend to be more stereotyped. They are:

- concrete sequential (CS);
- abstract sequential (AS);
- abstract random (AR); and
- concrete random (CR).

The instrument is easy to take and quick (about four minutes), contrasting with the Myers-Briggs, which takes forty-five minutes, then has to

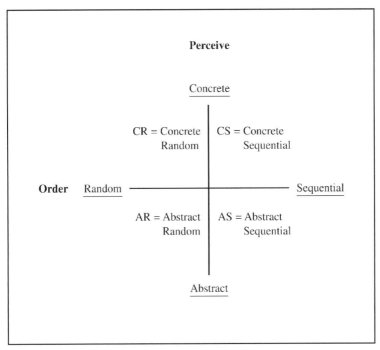

**Figure 3.1.   Structure of Gregorc Mind Styles Delineator**
*Source:* Anthony F. Gregorc, PhD

be scored by computer or by hand, and contains sixteen personality styles. The Gregorc, with only four major personality styles, is much easier to use. That also makes it easier to understand and to integrate into behavior.

Please note that these statements *tend* to be true of those with high scores, and so may be stereotypical.

## The Concrete Sequential Personality

This personality style (about 25 percent of the American population), often a loner, tends to:

- love order;
- make sure his/her desk is clean, uncluttered, neat;
- organize all kinds of things (even offering to organize your files);
- like details, facts, dealing with physical things;

- be a good student or employee, following directions literally;
- do one thing at a time, do it well, but not multitask;
- be task-oriented, meet deadlines;
- arrive early to classes and meetings; and
- love lists (actually finishes them), much to the surprise of the abstract randoms.

With extremely high scores (thirty-five and up on a forty-point scale), these patterns tend to be exaggerated. These tend to be draftsmen, book-keepers, architects, often in corrections, police, military, and fill adminis-trative positions because they are good doers, generally not intuitive, nor spontaneous. These occupations indicate that the CS is *a visual learner*.

How to work best with this personality?

- Present ideas about changing something on paper, with all details.
- Give him/her visuals (remember, we are dealing with *visual learners*).
- Don't waste his time with idle chatter.
- Focus on one item at a time—and avoid talking while he/she is reading or working on something.
- Do not sit at his/her desk which probably will offend him/her perma-nently, because he/she tends to be territorial, and becomes offended when his/her space is invaded.
- Expect him/her to hold grudges and to be critical, but thin-skinned per-sonally.

## The Abstract Random Personality

This warm, caring, emotional personality (about 50 to 60 percent of our population), who operates on a feeling level:

- hates hurting anyone's feelings;
- is a great friend, intensely loyal, makes hosts of friends—everywhere;
- does little planning, since is spontaneous, writes papers at the very last moment;
- likes loud parties and music, since is an *auditory learner*, usually not a visual learner;

- comes up with creative and intuitive ideas, solutions;
- is normally outgoing, extroverted, like Bette Midler, Auntie Mame, Dolly Parton;
- dresses colorfully, often flamboyantly; and
- Miss Congeniality in Miss America contests is almost always an AR.

Occupations? This personality likes working with people, public relations, helping professions, particularly in primary grades.

How can we work most effectively with this fun person, who enjoys life to the hilt? Easy.

- Abstract random personalities *love* to work in *groups* (the only style that does).
- They postpone doing something until the last moment.
- They have trouble with deadlines, staying on task, so need timetables with tasks spelled out.
- Avoid criticizing them; their feelings will be seriously hurt, because they interpret this as rejection and, consequently may shut down.
- Appreciate and respect this person's creativity and concern for people's feelings (since if we do not pay attention to the group's feelings it may come apart or become dysfunctional).
- The AR will look like he/she is having fun and certainly not focused, but work will get done—at the very last moment, exasperating the time-driven CSs.

## The Abstract Sequential Personality

This personality (3 to 5 percent of the population) lives in the world of ideas and concepts, and so can be a considerable asset to solving problems:

- are great analyzers, sometimes formidable synthesizers;
- are "big picture" people;
- often are sarcastic, feel superior, so are competitive, and thus loners;
- have big vocabularies;
- respect expertise, excellence, quality;
- personalities? Albert Einstein, Mr. Spock, Bill Gates;

- love lectures (nobody else does); and
- sometimes considered odd ducks.

Occupations? Professors of philosophy, psychology, scientists, attorneys, policy wonks.

How do you work with this relatively rare loner?

- Better be expert when you talk with her.
- Respect his "big picture" analyses and insights.
- Respect her looking at every side of problems, issues.
- Be patient with his tortured internal debates trying to decide on an issue (our daughter, Alana, is "so very annoyed with Hamlet because he is so unable to make decisions").

## The Concrete Random Personality

This person (15 to 25 percent of the population) has these personality traits:

- a risk-taker (Evil Knievel), so kids often get hurt physically with der-ring-do;
- troubleshooter, problem solver, inventor, innovator, entrepreneur (Thomas Edison, Donald Trump);
- often gifted mechanically—wants to take everything apart to see how it works, but too impatient to bother putting it together;
- autonomous—independence is their watchword ("don't fence me in"), so actually will leave a job if she feels hemmed in;
- loves challenges;
- jumps from project to project, has lots, usually unfinished;
- highly intuitive on little data;
- in school will do the first couple of problems, realizes that he/she can do them, so can't be bothered to finish—to parents' and math teachers' dismay;
- can't be threatened to be sent to the office, since usually can talk his/her way out of trouble;
- indifferent to rules/regulations, often feels challenged to violate some just to see reactions, or to see if he/she can get away with it; and
- very imaginative in getting around regulations.

Occupations? Work best when they are in charge or set agendas. Often self-employed.

How do you work with the CR?

- Give this loner her head.
- They are trial-and-error problem solvers, usually extremely creative, so are valuable group members.
- *Challenge* this personality by asking *if he really can pull solutions off*—and then let him work.
- He hates routine, so try to provide him with complex problems.

## Summary of Gregorc

Gregorc's instrument identifies four major personality styles and is easy to take, making an eminently practical and useful device. Our son, Marc, interviewed with a research organization, and said that the director had an abstract sequential personality like his, so he knew exactly how to work effectively with him—he was on target.

Many of us may be a combination of two personality styles, the most frequent being a person who has both concrete sequential and abstract random styles. This can be a considerable advantage because this person can work with details, paperwork, and yet be effective working with people—not a bad combination in education. Numerous guidance counselors are selected (or self-selected) for this combination.

Each personality is a gift—each has advantages and limitations. Effectively utilizing each with its numerous talents is necessary for organizations to thrive. A very astute principal, who has developed a team-taught constructivist school described in chapters 9 and 10, used the instrument in forming teams. It makes sense to have each style on a team. CS personalities focus on keeping people on task, are concerned about meeting deadlines, while ARs want to keep everyone happy attending to their emotional needs. The CR is going to be extremely creative with divergent solutions, while the AS is very much "big picture" in his/her approach to analyzing and solving problems.

Clearly, the Gregorc is an extremely useful tool in working with people—and with yourself since it is so descriptive, diagnostic, and predictive.

## KOHLBERG: STAGES OF MORAL REASONING

*Reflective Question*

*You might ask why on earth I'm including Kohlberg's (1981) stages of moral reasoning in a chapter giving cues regarding what makes us all tick. Ask no more.*

If we, as leaders, are able to use Kohlberg's ideas as a tool, we can evaluate the moral level upon which each student, colleague (including teachers, peer leaders, kids, superiors, relatives) are operating. Kohlberg's stages of moral reasoning are quite a tool, since they give us a heads-up on what to expect from each, providing essential information on how to interact with each.

Kohlberg came up with five stages of moral reasoning, to which Damon (1977) and Selmon (1980) added "0," prior to Kohlberg's first stage. Figure 3.2 illustrates these.

I recently was asked to evaluate a school in which the principal appeared to operate on stage 0. He was so power-mad that when my veteran wife heard how teachers described what he did to them ("attacked," "targeted," "harassed," "created a toxic environment," "poisonous," "suffering from posttraumatic stress disorder") she noted it sounded like a battlefield. His moral level appeared to be on the stage 0, egocentric reasoning, that is, "I *must* get my own way." At the opposite extreme, stage 5, are those for whom we have great respect, who appear to be on Maslow's self-actualized level.

1. Can you think of people who operate on this level, who have "the greatest respect for the rights and dignity of each person"?
2. On what level are teachers and colleagues whom you respect the most operating? Least?
3. How about top leaders in your organization? Who are easiest to work with? Most difficult?

I once started working as a department chairperson. I must have had some intuitive qualms about the head honcho, because I remember asking a friend whether the leader could be trusted. She said, "If you can't

| | | | |
|---|---|---|---|
| **Level I** | **STAGE 1:**<br>**UNQUESTIONING**<br>**OBEDIENCE**<br><br>(around kindergarten age) | WHAT'S RIGHT:<br><br>REASON TO<br>BE GOOD: | I should do what I'm told.<br><br>To stay out of trouble. |
| | **STAGE 2:**<br>**WHAT'S-IN-IT-**<br>**FOR-ME FAIRNESS**<br><br>(early elementary grades) | WHAT'S RIGHT:<br><br><br>REASON TO<br>BE GOOD: | I should look out for myself<br>but be fair to those who are<br>fair to me.<br><br>Self-interest: What's in it for me? |
| **Level II** | **STAGE 3:**<br>**INTERPERSONAL**<br>**CONFORMITY**<br><br>(middle-to-upper<br>elementary grades and<br>early-to-mid-teens) | WHAT'S RIGHT:<br><br><br>REASON TO<br>BE GOOD: | I should be a nice person and<br>live up to the expectations of<br>people I know and care about.<br><br>So others will think well of me<br>(social approval) and I can think<br>well of myself (self-esteem). |
| | **STAGE 4:**<br>**RESPONSIBILITY**<br>**TO "THE SYSTEM"**<br><br>(high-school years<br>or late teens) | WHAT'S RIGHT:<br><br><br>REASON TO<br>BE GOOD: | I should fulfill my responsibilities<br>to the social or value system I<br>feel part of.<br><br>To keep the system from falling<br>apart and to maintain self-<br>respect as somebody who<br>meets my obligations. |
| **Level III** | **STAGE 5:**<br>**PRINCIPLED**<br>**CONSCIENCE**<br><br>(young adulthood) | WHAT'S RIGHT:<br><br><br><br><br><br>REASON TO<br>BE GOOD: | I should show the greatest<br>possible respect for the rights<br>and dignity of every individual<br>person and should support a<br>system that protects human<br>rights.<br><br>The obligation of conscience to<br>act in accordance with the<br>principle of respect for all human<br>beings. |

**Figure 3.2. Kohlberg's Stages of Moral Reasoning**
*Source:* Stages of Moral Reasoning, pp. 176–77, table 2 from *Essays on Moral Development: The Philoso-
phy of Moral Development, Vol. I*, by Lawrence Kohlberg. Copyright © 1981 by Lawrence Kohlberg.
Reprinted by permission of HarperCollins Publishers.

trust him, whom can you trust?" Well, my intuition turned out on target. His memory became, oh, so conveniently forgetful at crucial points
when he said, "Oh, I don't remember that." Other chairpersons realized
that when we got to tight situations where we needed backing, it de-
pended on what he figured out was in it for him. His loyalty was zero.
On what level did he operate? It got to the point where I realized that
this situation could be dangerous, so I resigned after a couple of years.
No sense in setting myself up. On what levels are some business and

political leaders operating? Kenneth Lay of Enron? Your governor? Our presidents?

Kohlberg gives us a fascinating touchstone by which we can analyze behavior of our coworkers, family, and political and business leaders and establish expectations for their future behavior. How do they come out? How do you feel about it?

What can you do in dealing with those with whom you work? If you are working with someone operating on levels 0 or 1, he/she could be quite dangerous. People without a conscience become destroyers in organizations because they will use any means to get their way. Deutschman (2005) chillingly describes how psychopaths operate.

Do you see why I decided to use Kohlberg?

## GLASSER'S REALITY THERAPY

William Glasser, a psychiatrist, developed an approach in dealing with people, reality therapy (1975). Glasser sees two universal needs in all human beings. The need to love and to be loved is first, the second is to feel worthwhile to ourselves and to others. Glasser's approach is to focus on what works right now, in the immediate time. He laid out an eight-step approach to solving problems (below).

### Steps of Reality Therapy

1. Making friends.
   - Shake hands when you greet the client, smile, and make eye contact.
   - Lean forward and be attentive when listening, uncross arms, and keep eye contact.
   - Give at least two specific compliments about appearance, actions, or verbal statements.
   - Give compliments that only apply to the client.
   - Find at least two things that you have in common and spend time sharing them.
   - Tell a joke or humorous story.
   - Start a conversation with what you did this week instead of what they did—television, sports, parties, emotional highs and lows.

- Ask what the client does for fun and share what you do.
- Have specific things to talk about, that is, conversation pieces in your office, picture, plants, joke board, etc.
- Make a plan to do something together, that is, having lunch, playing a game, or going for a walk.
- Stay away from phones and note taking if possible.

2. What are you doing now? (present behavior)

- Ask questions only about what has happened in the past week.
- Go through the person's day, hour by hour and get through the whole day without making a plan to change.
- Ask how long it has been since you have done something, when you did it last, for how long you did this, and how many times.
- Ask at least three questions on any one subject area that may come up, for example, tennis: Where do you play? Who do you play with? What kind of racket do you use? etc.—before going on to the next area.

At intervals summarize back to the client the things he/she has told you. This reinforces the fact that you are interested in the client and what he/she does.

3. How is it helping? (evaluating present behavior)

- Ask if what they are doing now is helping their present situation.
- Ask for their value judgment before giving yours.
- Do not force or cheerlead the client into going in the direction you want him/her to go.
- Don't work yourself too hard. Get client to make value judgments.
- Review the problem in a very specific manner and then ask how those things the client is doing now are helping him.

4. Make a plan to do better.

- With a person whom you see as weak be sure not to ask "What can you do about your problem" or "What do you want to do about it?" but give them alternatives based on the information you got in step #2. You take control and be directive.
- Make a plan with the client which is:
  1. Simple: not complicated. A plan that the client will readily understand and be able to carry out.
  2. Specific: as to what, where, when, how many times, and how long.

3. To start something: make a plan which starts something rather than stops doing something. Example: to start giving one specific compliment to your secretary each day rather than putting her down less often.

4. Repetitive: something that can be repeated every day (or often) before your next meeting. Example: I'll smile and say "hello" to at least three people each day before noon.

5. Contingent on you: make a plan that is not contingent on others but only on what the client does or is going to do.

6. Immediate: something that can be started soon.

- Keep accurate records of plans

5. Get a commitment.

- Get client to say "I will do it"—not "I will try" or "Maybe I will do it."

- Discuss the commitment in a specific manner at the next meeting with the client, that is, tell me specifically what you did—more so than just did you do it or not.

6. Don't accept excuses.

- Cut off excuses as soon as they start.

- Confront the client about his excuses.

7. Don't punish: don't interfere with reasonable consequences.

- Talk specifically about the natural consequences (positive or negative) of all alternatives.

- Do not inflict the consequences without talking about the rules or consequence first.

- Allow certain natural consequences to occur.

8. Don't give up.

- Make a plan for the client to come back even though you don't know where therapy is going.

- Call the client up to see how he/she is doing.

- Hang in there longer than the client thinks you will.

Reality therapy (RT) encourages making a plan and dealing with an issue(s) immediately. It avoids fixing blame and complaining, focuses instead on developing solutions. Note who takes responsibility: the individual.

In RT, therapist and client build a support system where they focus on helping and supporting the individual. The therapist's role is to facilitate the individual solving his issues by making *a plan* so that both can see results immediately. Thus, the individual develops a plan, which identifies the problem or situation, but also becomes responsible for taking immediate action to resolve the situation.

You might argue, "OK, this seems useful for individuals, but we work with groups of kids, with faculties, with administrators and leaders. How can we use this with our groups?" Again, this becomes a lot easier when we put our fertile minds to it. Why not psych out the process Glasser uses and apply it to social systems with which we are working?

What are his eight elements? Again, look at figure 3.2. It makes sense to make friends with the person(s), since we virtually cannot get anywhere with anyone unless we establish a *relationship* (which usually involves developing mutual trust [see chapter 11]). I'm involved presently with collective negotiations over our contract, where it is essential to establish positive relationships with the "other side," since we are involved in an enterprise which absolutely requires that we cooperate to achieve our goals, even though we obviously have some different interests. But our joint goal is to get something that is somewhat satisfying to each.

Notice the focus on developing a practical plan and looking at results for each step. My therapist wife often asks me, "What is this behavior getting you?" Sometimes, answering this is exasperatingly annoying, because I have to look at what I'm doing and try to be objective. The question is certainly on target. If behavior is getting results that we do not like, it's time to change it.

In organizations, this is a bit more complicated. What to do? Do we have a solution for you! Just look at chapter 9, on diagnosing a school, for a useful model. I've used it for reforming elementary, middle, and high schools.

Conclusion: Glasser's principles can be used to deal with individuals, as well as with groups and organizations. The chapter 9 model is a take-off on Glasser's ideas (by establishing a plan, building support systems, establishing relationships, etc.) and Kurt Lewin (1952a), and, as befits the complexity of a school, is itself complex—but exceedingly useful.

## GEORGE HERBERT MEAD'S SYMBOLIC INTERACTION

Who? Symbolic interaction? Have I lost my mind (a question often asked by my amused wife)? Here's the background. George Herbert Mead was a close friend of John Dewey at the University of Chicago, where he probably was a major early source of Dewey's philosophy (Professor E. V. Johanningmeier, personal communication, March 3, 2005). Oh, by the way, Mead founded contemporary social psychology.

What is it? How can I/we use it? Mead focused on two essential elements of being human: the formation of the "self" and the "act," how we act toward each other, both emerging from our living in society and interacting with each other. While this doesn't seem too profound, it is what distinguishes Mead's thinking about human behavior and what differs from most psychologists, where they treat the individual as *an individual*, not as *a member of a society* in which individuals act together. And, it is a major base for understanding constructivism and its uses because the self is formed through reciprocal relationships, which Lambert et al. (1995) hold is the basis for developing constructivist leadership. See chapter 11 for a full discussion of her basic insight, which, essentially, presents a comprehensive theory and practice of constructivist leadership.

### The Self (Which Is What Makes Us Human)

Mead sees the *self* as emerging from the fact that we treat ourselves *as an object*. That is, we *interact* with ourselves.

*Reflective Question*

*For example, do you ever have an internal conversation with yourself?*

Tennis players do this a lot, when they castigate themselves after a goof, muttering "Was that stupid!" or some other pleasant compliment. Another example usually occurs after a driver cuts us off, or pulls some dumb stunt. Have you ever muttered to yourself, "What a dumb stunt!"?

By interacting with ourselves, we've demonstrated that we have a self. And the self acts as an intervening mechanism between us and things happening in the world. For example, if we are hungry do we immediately race around eating anything in sight? We deal with the pangs by looking at a variety of options, such as thinking about going out, holding off until we finish a task, or deciding to ask a coworker if she wants to go someplace, etc. In other words, we interact with our selves; we do not immediately jump into action as the stimulus-response (S-R) brand of psychology believes.

How is the self formed? Mead pointed to three stages:

1. A baby begins to imitate daddy reading the paper (but holds it upside down)—about one to three years of age.
2. The child takes one of two roles: "I'll be the mommy, you be the baby." Or the child constructs another scenario with two roles: "Let's have lunch. I'll make it and you eat it" (the food and drink are often imaginary). Note that at this stage of the development of the self, only two roles are involved and the child only takes one role at a time—about three to six or seven years of age.

   How can you see this demonstrated? Easy. Have you ever seen four- or five- or even six-year-olds play baseball? What happens when a ball is hit into the outfield? All the little kids run to get the ball, much to their parents' dismay. Since the kids can only take one role at a time, they do not understand adults' expectations for their position, even when adults express paroxysms of agony (read, screaming directions) to very confused kids. At that age kids have not grasped the idea that there are different expectations for each position's role.
3. Starting at about six or seven years of age, kids slowly begin to be able to deal with more than one role at a time. That is, they begin to learn norms (read, customs) and expectations for each role. In baseball, they learn that each position has different expectations for how it is played. Mead called this the "generalized other."

Now, let's look at the mechanics of how the self is formed (and this is why Mead is a *social psychologist*). He pointed out that each of us develops a self through our perceptions, our interpretations, of others' reactions to us. Very simply, that explains why we aren't logical animals (like Mr. Spock and the Vulcans). If a person has had an abusive childhood, merely pointing out that his behavior is illogical will not make much difference. We see the illogic. But, the person is immersed in his perceptions of his self, is locked inside his own skin. The problem has to be worked out emotionally, hardly a logical process. This explains why objective help from the outside, such as a friend or a counselor, perhaps using RT, often is necessary to "get outside of our own skin" for an objective assessment of our behavior.

In the heading for this section, I've indicated that developing a self is what makes us human, implying that this is an exclusive property of us *Homo sapiens*. But have we any research (not common sense) about any animals that indicates that they have developed a self? Oddly, we do. Koko, the gorilla, who has been taught American Sign Language, seems to have developed a self. Koko can sign such sentences as, "Koko hungry," "Koko sad," Koko happy," "Koko want baby." Koko is talking about herself, treating herself as an object. Note that she is carrying on a conversation about herself and her needs. When she sees herself in a mirror, she notes that the person there is Koko. Presently, we do not have evidence that monkeys do that. When they look in a mirror, they think it is another monkey.

## THE ACT

*Reflective Questions*

*1. Why on earth are we talking about the act?*
*2. Everyone acts, so what's so special?*

It is the basic unit of human behavior. All behavior is an act (except for reflex actions, such as being startled, sneezing, etc.). Each act we do is built up as we interact with ourselves. While we wake up with a start when the alarm goes off (which is a reflex action), everything after that becomes an act. We have to decide whether to keep on sleeping and hit the snooze button, or whether to look at the clock if it's a weekday, or whether to leap out of bed, or whether to make coffee first or go the bathroom, or whether. . . . We have lots of options. Each of these possibilities goes into our making a decision about what to do—into what becomes one act. Thus, the act is built up, consists of lots of possibilities, about which we make decisions. Certainly, we make a lot of them fast, because we think very quickly. Note we're doing this all by ourselves, all alone.

Now, how about when we interact with others? Ok, when we interact with others, we react to our *interpretations* of their words, of their facial expressions, of their body signals. We *imagine* their *intentions*. If we're on target, generally it's because we have *shared or common meanings* and can develop joint action. If we misunderstand their communication, their intentions, we generate difficulties. We were talking last night with a Thai and American couple, who run a Thai restaurant, about communication misunderstandings. Although they've been married seven years, he indicated that this occurs. Because the Thai language does not have a word for "please," when his wife asks him to do something, it often comes across as an order, so it gets his back up. This still occurs after seven years.

So, we interpret each other's meanings from their acts, we *infer* their intentions. Our acts, actions, are more complex, because we tune in so carefully to read the real meanings people are expressing in their behavior. Obviously, we become expert at looking for patterns in behavior, including ours. The movie *What the Bleep Do We Know?* (2004) supports this from the viewpoint of quantum physics.

Clearly, the fundamental unit of the personality, the self, is profoundly impacted by our surrounding culture. Chapters 4 and 5 deal with culture and the organization. For example, about 60 percent of Americans are abstract random and only about 25 percent of us are concrete sequential, while approximately 75 percent of Finns tend to be concrete sequential.

*Reflective Question*

*How can we use all this?*

Certain personalities (the extreme concrete sequential [CS] and abstract sequential [AS] personalities) might become too rigid in playing out roles. I can think of a mother with high CS scores in a workshop the other day telling us that she has been pressuring her concrete random, very creative son to change his random behavior of developing lots of projects—with absolutely no effect. She's been pressuring him for ten years. That's pretty rigid. We asked her how long it would take her to change her behavior, realize that it was useless to pressure him. She did not like hearing that.

The highly flexible extreme randoms (concrete randoms [CR] and abstract randoms [AR]) might need to focus more, with the people-person AR deciding not to give in to please the world. One needs to stand one's ground at times (again, note that the act is complex and is the result of interpretations of our own and others' intentions).

Do you have to or want to form teams, committees? Make sure that you have at least one person from each style on it for balance. The CS will make sure that tasks and timetables will be adhered to. The AR will make sure that people's feelings are listened to and that creative approaches will be developed. The AS will come up with big-picture solutions and the CR will create clever, often way-out, but practical solutions.

## CALVIN TAYLOR'S FAMILIES OF TALENTS

*Reflective Question*

*What is the advantage of perceiving everyone as having talents?*

If we look at people as having bundles or families of talents, Taylor (1968) noted, of course, that 50 percent are above average in that one talent. If we take two talents, the percent above average will be likely to be in the high 60s. Across several talents, 90 percent will be above average. Obviously, this is a fascinating way to view people, since we start looking for their talents—and treat everyone as above average!

Taylor lists families of talents, to which we can add others:

- academic;
- creative;
- communication;
- planning;
- decision making;
- physical (athletics, dance);
- forecasting/predicting;
- entrepreneurial; and
- analyzing/synthesizing.

What others can you think of?

In using this concept, we suddenly perceive people—everyone—as talented. The key is to look for individuals' talents that can be developed.

Suddenly, everyone is above average—we can change from focusing on people's deficits to looking for their positives—their families of talents.

## MCCLELLAND AND ACHIEVEMENT MOTIVATION (NACH)

McClelland (1961) developed the achievement motivation construct, which is pretty self-evident once we think about it. Western society places a great value on people who are motivated to achieve by recognizing many kinds of achievement. High schools reflect this value with such rituals as ranking students by their grades (class rank), Honor Society admissions, most popular student, athletic banquets, etc. A number of instruments and workshops have been developed using this idea.

## SUMMARY

So, what makes Terry tick?

Her personality.
Her background.
Her needs (Maslow's hierarchy of needs):
- physiological
- safety
- social
- esteem
- aesthetic
- self-actualization

We briefly looked into our needs for power and control over running our lives, and discussed the nature of power very briefly (see chapter 8).

Gregorc provides fascinating insights into four different mind styles, the concrete sequential, abstract random, abstract sequential, and concrete random personalities.

Next, Kohlberg's insights into moral stages of development can be extremely useful in working with people. A question I sometimes ask in dealing with someone who displays unusual behavior patterns is whether he/she has a conscience. That's very important to consider in our interaction, because if that person does not have one, he is capable of almost anything and will generate huge problems in your organization and to you.

Glasser tells us how to get individuals and groups on track to deal with some of their problems and issues by forming a plan, taking immediate action, and then getting feedback from objective persons.

George Herbert Mead digs into how our personality, our self, is formed, and how we learn the fundamental roles we play in life and in society. And he sheds light on the complex way we interact with ourselves and with others as we interpret our own and others' intentions as our acts develop and are built. Obviously, Mead provides a fundamental underpinning of constructivism, discussed in chapters 9, 10, and 11. Last, Calvin Taylor and David McClelland add to our armamentarium of different ways to perceive people: Taylor that we have numerous bundles of talents, providing opportunities to expand and to use those talents, and McClelland that many people have a strong drive to achieve.

## GLOSSARY

**Gregorc's Personality Style Delineator**   a practical instrument pointing out four major personality styles.

**Kohlberg's stages of moral reasoning**   a model of stages of moral development.

**Glasser's reality therapy**   an eight-step approach to solving human problems.

**George Herbert Mead's symbolic interaction**   a social psychological approach to understanding how humans interact and form the self through reciprocal relationships.

*Section III*

# MORE TOOLS: THE DYNAMICS OF ORGANIZATIONS AND CONSTRUCTIVIST LEADERSHIP

Good organizations are like ducks; they look calm on the surface, but are paddling like hell underneath.

—Anonymous

*Chapter Four*

# What Makes Organizations (Read, Schools) Tick?

## A Quick Guide to How Organizations Work

Some kids know how to operate in organizations, and some kids have no idea of what to do and how to do it. So, they can't avoid getting into trouble—so, they become victims.

—Alana and Marc Shapiro, when they were teenagers

*Reflective Questions*

*1. Why should we in leadership study how **organizations** function?*
*2. Don't we know that?*

The preceding chapter gave us some insight into what makes people tick because if we do not understand ourselves and our colleagues, we simply will be ineffective in working with them. Similarly, if we do not understand thoroughly how organizations function, we will succeed only by being really lucky. And we cannot count on luck to bail us out all the time. To put it starkly, we cannot be successful without understanding *how organizations operate*. Some tragic, career-destroying examples exist of principals forgetting this in their haste to move rapidly once they assume that they hold the reins of power.

Actually, we live, we swim in a sea, an ocean, of organizations virtually every day, every hour, and every minute of our lives. We are awakened by a radio broadcasting from a station (an organization), we eat cereal manufactured and distributed by organizations, we listen to an organization (the police) informing us of traffic jams on our way to work in our organization's building, we drive there in a car built by another organization, serviced by an organization. . . . So, even our day starts with numerous organizations, some subtly and others directly impacting us.

This chapter deals with some major aspects of the **structure** of organizations, including **positions, roles, role expectations**, and their virtually inevitable conflict, because we occupy a variety of roles in our personal and professional lives. We also deal with such factors as **hierarchy** and **authority**, coming up with some startling insights, which are extremely important for us to function effectively in our organizational lives. Next, we deal with another major component of the structure of organizations, that we inevitably create **social systems** (groups), while guided by **customs** or **norms**, and a **subculture** and **climate** as we live in our organizations. Chapter 5, on hidden behavior, completes this third section of the book on what makes organizations tick by digging into key hidden and highly influential behavior that lurks below the surface, the hidden images, cycles, and pulls that control our thinking and behavior as we mush through our organizations.

In section IV, chapter 6 deals with the essential need for and strategies for developing a purpose. Chapter 7 focuses on strategies to establish ourselves and chapter 8 provocatively lays out differing, but key formulations of power, authority, and influence for the practitioner.

## A KEY UNIVERSAL ELEMENT: STRUCTURE

*Reflective Questions*

1. *Have you ever sat back and asked what are the key elements every organization in our society displays, even the informal ones like families and friendship groups?*
2. *What are they?*

If we examine organizations very carefully, we see that they are manmade entities. As a matter of fact, sociologists consider them *socially constructed realities*—one of the things we do in organizations when they start is create structures immediately.

For example, if you bet that all organizations develop a structure, even as they start, you can take your winnings to the bank. Just look at organizations—any one. Your school has a principal, teachers, students, custodians, perhaps cafeteria workers, and if large enough, an assistant principal or two, often a counselor. And, let's not forget the students, who develop student councils, honor societies, clubs, teams, and on and on.

Police departments have structures (patrolmen, sergeants, lieutenants, captains), as do our local stores (manager, clerks), and the local library. So do the U.S. Marines, as does the local church, temple, or synagogue (minister or priest or rabbi, secretary, members, president of the parishioners, etc.). Whenever I go into an organization, I want to know the structure, since it tells me who is responsible to whom, crucial in working effectively with any organization.

*Reflective Question*

*Now, what do you think are the universal elements of these organizational structures?*

## UNIVERSAL ELEMENTS: ALL ORGANIZATIONS CREATE POSITIONS AND ROLES—THEIR BUILDING BLOCKS

### Charlie Brown as Manager and Pitcher—and Loser

When any organization is created, we think immediately of different *positions* necessary to run it. When Charlie Brown gets his baseball team together, he always takes the manager's position (where he becomes somewhat of a wimp, to be sure); at the same time, he sets up his role as pitcher, too, another position. And the different characters literally take different positions (outfielder, first baseman). If a restaurant opens up near you, it always has a manager, cooks, hostesses, usually cashiers and servers, and you, the customer.

Even informal organizations, such as our families or clubs, create positions. Two adults can create a family. When and if children arrive, they occupy considerably different positions than adults. Grandparents have different positions than parents, different than uncles and aunts.

Sociologists also call positions *statuses*, which differs from *prestige*. Prestige is allocated in different amounts to various positions. Obviously, ministers have more prestige than choirboys and choir directors, as does the principal in comparison with her teachers, and they, in turn, with their pupils. Sergeant majors have much more prestige in their position than privates.

The next critical element is the *role*. A role consists of a *series of expectations* for a position—any position (Gross, Mason, and McEachern 1966). And expectations differ, so that one can be a passive, laissez-faire principal, another person can act out his role as a bureaucrat, still another as a faculty or student advocate, still another principal can develop a different set of expectations as . . . (you fill this in). The point is that roles for positions can differ according to various expectations different groups develop for that status, as well as those that the person in the position develops.

Thus, *how* a person acts out a status becomes his/her role. Charlie Brown creates a hapless role as a manager. As a football kicker, his role invariably is that of a sucker for Lucy. Lucy always takes the role of the wiseass. Interestingly, both their roles are fairly stable, generally true of roles people develop and sustain. Note, then, that the role we develop consists of our understanding and acting out of one series of the expectations surrounding it. It comprises our *interpretation* of how that position should be implemented. Others might carry them out differently.

## INTERESTINGLY, AS ROLE EXPECTATIONS DEVELOP, THEY CAN CREATE ROLE CONFLICT

### Charlie Brown and Phil Jackson

It is pretty obvious that different clusters of role expectations can develop for each position in an organization. While Charlie Brown expects to be an inept manager (and pitcher, too), Phil Jackson, formerly manager of the world champion Chicago Bulls, and then of the Los Angeles Lakers basketball teams, functioned quite differently. He expected his teams to win. A novelty among coaches, his interpretation bordered on a Zen role. I once saw a coach being highly stressed out and remarked to a dean who had been a former coach that the man on television was so wild. The dean noted, "That's his choice."

For principals, a series of different role expectations can be seen and sometimes heard, often according to which important **reference group** you focus on. Superintendents want reports in on time, their expectation for the principal's role. Most teachers want to be treated with consideration and compassion. Often, parents want control and for their kids to get high test scores. The union does not want teachers to be hassled. Fellow principals expect a principal to look, dress, and act confidently. The board of education wants principals to look professional and to follow policies.

## Reference Groups/Social Systems and Role Conflict—Not Funny

Each of these groups is essentially a *reference group*, or a *social system*, toward which principals have to keep a weather eye, in order to satisfy them. It is sometimes a tall order, to which any principal can attest. And, therein lies the rub.

The principal new to his/her role has to tack through the various conceptions of the role in order to survive, let alone prosper—often a difficult proposition. My comments above regarding each reference group or social system's expectations are somewhat simplified, since reference groups often have a variety of expectations among their members, often conflicting, to define the role of the principal.

Thus, role expectations take time to ferret out as one lives in organizations. People from the outside often are unaware of the welter of conflicting expectations from each social system, a reason why educational leaders with no experience as teachers or administrators so often fail. They fail to pick up the riptides, the underwater currents, the hidden shoals of expectations that each social system holds for leaders. And failure to pick up those undercurrents can lead to severe disappointments to key social systems—even loss of their support.

Examples abound. Sometimes, new teachers may expect principals to help them with their organization or with the discipline of classes, and may approach principals openly and trustingly. More veteran teachers, possibly burned by previous administrators, do not want to draw attention, may distrust the principal, keeping their distance warily (both social and spatial), waiting to see how he/she operates. We will deal with the absolutely crucial role of trust and distrust in chapter 11. Some teachers may want principals to treat everyone equally, while others may want differential treatment (being able to take time to take care of their kids, to go to a physician or dentist during school hours). These provide administrators with crisp examples of **role conflict**.

As for parents, some may want their kids to be treated as special (National Honor Society, elite, advanced, ability-grouped classes [particularly true of upper-middle-class parents]), while others may want all kids treated alike and avoid contending with fallout from tracking. So, life for principals is not a bowl of cherries. Note that teachers also have widely differing expectations for such issues as ability grouping and tracking.

## Guba and Getzels's Contributions to Understanding Role Conflict

So, different expectations arise from the same social system or reference group. Guba and Getzels (1957) addressed this in their famous model, later modified by Thelen (Getzels and Thelen 1960). See fiure 4.1.

Observing people interacting in organizations, they saw two dimensions of behavior. The first, the **nomothetic**, consists of the organization developing various roles, illustrated by clusters of expectations, which are developed in order to achieve the organization's goals. The second, Guba

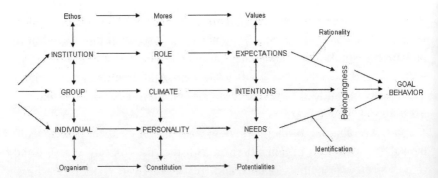

**Figure 4.1.   Getzel and Guba's Social Behavior and Administrative Process**
Source: J. W. Getzels and H. A. Thelen, "The classroom group as a unique social system," *Yearbook of the National Society for the Study of Education* 59, no. 2 (1960): 53–82.

and Getzels called the **idiographic dimension**, consisting of the individual's personality predispositions, which consist of individual's needs. Figure 4.1 illustrates these dimensions.

Guba and Getzels, in their effort to understand how individuals and organizations operate, stated, "To understand the behavior of specific role incumbents in an institution, we must know both the role-expectations and the need-dispositions. Indeed, needs and expectations may be thought of as motives for behavior, the one driving from personal propensities, the other from institutional requirements." Later, they added, "A given act is conceived as deriving simultaneously from both the nomothetic and the idiographic dimensions. . . . [S]ocial behavior results as the individual attempts to cope with the environment composed of patterns of expectations for his behavior in ways consistent with his own independent patterns of needs" (Guba and Getzels 1957, 52–54).

## Interpretation: My Conflicting Internal Expectations for My Role

What are they saying? The value of this model is that it points out conflict that may occur in any person and in any organization, caused by different expectations we have for roles personally and professionally. A principal may want to be caring, yet has to evaluate teachers doing a poor job, failing to meet his/her own expectations for the position. These are conflicting role expectations each person may hold.

"Tough love" provides a crystal clear example of role conflict by a person who faces the trauma of turning a child over to the police for illegal drug use and yet desperately loves the child. What to do? This illustrates the pain any of us may face when we enable someone. We suddenly realize that our behavior is essentially crippling the person by permitting him to continue his dysfunctional behavior.

In actuality, extreme forms of internal role conflict within oneself are the stuff of high drama, although rare. When Greek King Oedipus unknowingly marries his own mother, the former queen, and finds out, he is torn by conflict. He literally cannot bear to see the role conflict caused by being the husband of his own mother, two horrendously conflicting roles. In the play, he blinds himself.

## INTERPRETATION: MY VARIOUS ROLES IN CONFLICT

*Reflective Questions*

*1. What role conflicts do you face in your professional practice?*
*2. Which are conflicts among the various roles you play?*

Next, we can look at conflicting expectations faced by the principal in his/her organizational roles. She may want to be perceived by her own personal kids as caring and loving, and yet has role expectations to have high expectations for performance for the secretary and for teachers and may have to replace them. We see her two roles in conflict.

We next can view role expectations from two different social systems. The faculty might expect the principal to suspend the football team's seventeen-year-old honor-student kicker for drinking beer on a skiing trip (his rule-enforcing role), while the parents might want a more merciful decision—and threaten legal action for suspension. It can get even more complicated when he realizes that suspending the student might cause the team to lose the game with a fellow principal's team with whom he made a friendly bet about wearing that team's jersey in school the next Monday if his team lost.

We often are caught between a number of not-so-obvious conflicting expectations, which Guba and Getzels clearly pointed out. For example, of late, the high-stakes testing mania has placed many between the grinding teeth of wanting their kids to do well and the ethical necessity of letting happen what may happen. Some people have tried to help their students, destroying their teaching careers.

Other illustrations may help us understand the contributions of this model. Numbers of administrators are succumbing to pressuring their staffs to set a goal of increasing testing scores. Yet, many note that kids may do best by going about the business of learning without being taught to the test, as Isaacson discovered when her entire school moved into constructivist teaching (Isaacson 2004). See chapter 9. Benjamin (1989), in a prescient article, predicted this outcome as we began to shudder into the testing movement.

## THE NEXT COMPONENT OF STRUCTURE: HIERARCHY AND AUTHORITY

### Hierarchy

When we create our organizations, we inevitably create positions. Almost inevitably, we place some positions above others in terms of having more power, authority, prestige, respect. In other words, we create a hierarchy of positions, some having more worth—and more power—than others. One reason for this is that organizations may work better in certain respects if the concept of division of labor is used. Even in the family, we use that idea. For example, in a traditional family, the wife may do the cooking, but may expect the husband to take out the garbage and to barbecue on the grill outdoors. In a more contemporary family, division of labor may not be as pronounced, and in some cases, roles may reverse, with husbands staying home to care for kids.

In more formal organizations, the director of medicine in a hospital has more authority and prestige than nurses or admitting clerks. Superintendents of schools have more authority than do bus drivers, meaning that he or she can make decisions that generally will stick over a considerably wider area than the driver. Boards of education have greater authority than even superintendents, since in most states they hire that person, and generally are expected to establish policies, which superintendents are expected to carry out.

### Authority

While the concept of hierarchy is pretty clear, that of *authority* is murkier, since there are a number of ways to look at it (see chapter 8 for further discussion of its relationship with power). Much of Western thinking has been affected by our several thousands of years of belief that authority is top-down. That is, we thought that authority came down from God to the king and then down to princes and down the line until we reached serfs, who almost literally had no authority to order anyone about (except wives and kids, if they had them).

Barnard (1938) changed that notion forever when he laid out four conditions for a subordinate to *accept* the authority of a person's order.

1. The first condition is that subordinates must be able to understand the communication.
2. The second condition for accepting a directive is the person must feel that it conforms to the purposes of the organization.
3. The third condition is that the individual must believe that the order fits in with his/her own personal value system.
4. The fourth condition is that he or she must be able to carry it out mentally and physically.

Let's see how this formulation plays out.

The first point is clear, since if we do not understand or perceive what the communication is all about, we cannot follow it. The second gets into the head of the subordinate. If he or she perceives or believes that the communication is counter to the purposes of the organization, we get a good deal of conflict, and probably fear. It's not easy to question a superior about a directive to do something without paying a penalty, which could include losing a job. All of a sudden, we have a more complex situation on our hands with Barnard's second point.

The third point Barnard makes is also tricky. A cousin of mine asked a number of his fellow soldiers during one of our wars if they could shoot someone. A goodly number of them indicated that that would be very hard to do—and the research bore this finding out. The role of the whistle-blower fits this point very well. We have had several cases of whistle-blowers emerging in major scandals, such as Enron, the case of the FBI missing vital information that field agents e-mailed regarding 9/11, etc. We even have legislation nationally that whistle-blowers are not to be attacked, although this does not seem to deter some.

The last point made by Barnard is self-evident. When we lived on the side of a hill in Nashville, Tennessee, if I had asked my then nine-year-old son to mow the lawn, he simply could not do it. It was difficult enough for an adult.

Now, let's see what Barnard has done with this formulation. First of all, Barnard has converted our thinking about authority into concentrating about *communicating*. Note that he focuses on the *subordinate accepting a communication.* Barnard has changed our way of thinking about authority as something absolute into perceiving authority as a communication from a superior to a subordinate that is accepted! Essentially, we are dealing with *the process of communication* with this formulation, a major change in our thinking.

## IS OUR AUTHORITY BASED ON COMMUNICATION?

*Reflective Question*

*Is communication really the basis of authority?*

If Barnard is accurate, authority is now in the realm of *perception* of communication. In short, if I do not *accept* your communication, do you have authority? This comprises a 180-degree turnaround in thinking from viewing authority as coming from above, the king, to perceiving it as being *accepted by subordinates.*

A teacher/friend of mine became so fed up with a nit-picking chairman in her high school, that, much to his astonishment, she told him she wouldn't accept his authority any more. And, she didn't. This shoved him into quite a quandary, since I was the superintendent, and she was perceived correctly as a family friend. Eventually, he began to mend his ways since other faculty began to react negatively to his pickiness and high needs for control.

## ANOTHER UNIVERSAL STRUCTURAL ELEMENT: ALL ORGANIZATIONS CREATE SOCIAL SYSTEMS—WHAT MAKES THEM TICK

### Cliques Are Social Systems

*Reflective Questions*

*1. What do you think and feel when you hear the word "clique"?*
*2. Write five words about cliques on a separate piece of paper.*
*3. Are most negative? Why?*

Generally—we react adversely. We believe that cliques exclude us, that they're formed of people who do not want to let us into "their" group, their territory. Actually, Webster's dictionary supports this, calling it "a narrow exclusive circle or group of persons; especially one held together by common interests, views or purposes."

But is this valid, or just a result of years of being uncomfortable in our assumed notion that the clique may not let us in? Or is it that we think that they're not our kind of people, with whom we would want to hang around, as Groucho Marx famously noted?

Whatever it is, cliques seem to have developed fairly negative reactions. They almost come across as the term, "gang." If we switch terms and use the words "social system" instead, which is what social scientists such as sociologists call small groups in organizations, we suddenly have a tool to look at *the fundamental, the basic unit* of any organization. We are able to drop our less-than-positive-images and attitudes simply by changing the term. (This may become a technique to use as we think about how to improve our functioning in our daily professional behavior and practice.)

Social systems are the basic units of all groups, of all organizations. That is, organizations are composed of a whole series of small groups of people who hang together. What I'm saying is that the social system is the fundamental unit of structure in all organizations (Barnard 1938; Parsons and Shills 1951; Lammers 1987; Reed and Hughes 1992; Bausch 2001).

As a matter of fact, we are quite astute in watching who associates with whom in our organizations. We do this by watching who has lunch with whom, who talks with whom, who seems to want to work with each other—and, we note it carefully.

## THE FAMILY IS A SOCIAL SYSTEM

*Reflective Questions*

1. *Does the idea of social systems apply to families?*
2. *Which kids seem to like to work together (if you have more than a single kid)?*
3. *Who sides with whom in arguments? Who is the favorite of each parent?*
4. *Who wants to go with whom when we do things together?*

We have a lot of blended families. How careful are newish parents to treat everyone fairly? Is there a Cinderella? If so, what is the unspoken, the hidden curriculum in this family? Everyone can be damaged because the unspoken message is that it's OK to discriminate in this family, it's OK to pick on someone. Attitudes give clear messages. Kids will bring this hidden curriculum into their schools. So will teachers and administrators who come from families with these hidden beliefs.

## Social Systems in Our Organizations

The same applies to all our organizations, such as faculty meetings, committees, work groups, etc. The astute principal will know quickly which people will want to work together on a project, just as the sensitive teacher will be able to predict which kids will want to work together—and who absolutely should not. (If you're going for a higher degree make absolutely—no, positively—certain that the people you ask to work on your committee like and respect each other—or, your committee meetings will resemble a war with the members fighting each other, while you watch helplessly, and you may become a casualty, a truly unpleasant outcome— for you!)

We must be sensitive to alliances people make with each other in order to work effectively, or we really will be operating blindly. If we cannot figure out those alliances, who likes and dislikes each other, who trusts and distrusts each other, we'll produce unneeded conflict. Key tasks either will not get done, or will sop up too much of our social capital (which is never unlimited). So, picking up on who wants to work with whom, who doesn't trust whom, is absolutely essential to being effective.

We've pretty well clarified how to recognize a social system when we meet one. Simply put, a social system is any two or more people interacting meaningfully (Guba and Getzels 1957). We are startled when we start to figure out how many social systems a group of only five people generates. Ten dyads (read, twos), six triads (read, threes), five social systems of four people, and the five itself is a social system. This totals twenty-two different social systems. Just trying to calculate the number of social systems in a small faculty of twenty or twenty-five people boggles the mind.

But we are pretty astute. We usually can figure out key reference groups in a faculty, and know which person to go to in order to get different things done. Chapter 7, on how to establish yourself, expands dealing with social systems.

## UNIVERSAL ELEMENTS: NORMS (READ, CUSTOMS) AND DELIBERATELY CREATING A POSITIVE CULTURE

As people in their social systems work and associate together, they develop expectations of each other's behavior. My kids would not start eating at Thanksgiving until their grandmother stopped caroming around the kitchen and sat down to eat. She, to give her credit, respected their custom, and would sit down to start off the meal. We generally are quite unaware that we develop so many norms in our daily and professional lives. We were in a Dairy Queen, a family restaurant, when an older adolescent started using very foul language (there were very young children there). One of our friends told him in no uncertain terms that it was very bad form to curse in front of the youngsters. The adolescent stopped violating the norms.

Note that behavior can be both acceptable and unacceptable simultaneously. His language might have been OK for his peers, but not for a family. And, now we can see that patterns of norms become part of the **culture** of any society and group. In short, as we interact, we develop patterns of shared, learned behavior that we use in connection with living with others, a culture (Linton 1955). Everyone in a culture learns these patterns of shared expectations, which we pass on to youngsters. We generally do not have to tell six-year-olds not to bite other kids. They learn that early on. We all learn commonly expected and accepted ideas, values, attitudes, and habits as we grow up in a society and a culture.

It is only when we hit another culture that we become aware of our own cultural norms, as, for example, when my son and I went to an Ethiopian restaurant in Washington, D.C. First of all, tables were even lower than knee height sitting down, so you have to lean forward to eat. Then, since utensils are not cultural artifacts in that country, you have to tear off a piece of soft bread and pick up the food to eat it; however, they had napkins to wipe our fingers.

*Reflective Question*

*Can you think of any examples of cultural differences, such as food, language, buying habits, or regional differences, in our country that you have come across?*

For example, Americans have breakfast foods, while some cultures do not, eating the same foods for all three or five meals. How about clambakes in New England, and the focus on corn dishes in the Midwest? The South has grits, which Northerners often put maple syrup on, to the dismay of waitresses.

Our son wrote on returning from a visit to Asia a list of "the top 15 differences one notices upon returning to the United States from Nepal and India." Among them are:

1. White, peaked mountains, glacial lakes, 500 seasonal foot waterfalls and yak trains generally not considered pedestrian, commonplace sights.
2. Relatively few cows hanging around in the middle of the road, grazing in one's neighborhood, around major tourist destinations, roaming through bus and train stations, waiting next to you on the train platform . . . heck, everywhere. . . .
3. Beasts of burden, such as buffalo, oxen, and camels are considered fairly uncommon modes of transporting freight along the streets of most major American cities.

## Developing Subcultures and Climates

All we have to do to pick up on *subcultures* is to head to different parts of our country. I once asked a native-born Southern friend of mine if his mother, who was preparing dinner, was making Southern-fried chicken. He looked stunned, and really considered it bordering on being idiotic, but was polite (somewhat). He asked me what other fried chicken there was. Two friends seriously considered moving to Florida, but gave it up after realizing that the clambakes they loved in Connecticut would then belong to a former life.

Organizations, too, develop subcultures. Compare and contrast the subculture of an elementary school with that of a bank. Typically, banks present a relatively formal front to us customers, whereas the people in an elementary school are usually friendly and like the little people who bop around very seriously. Often, such schools are pretty informal—and very busy.

Owens (1998, 165) notes that

> culture refers to the behavioral norms, assumptions, and beliefs of an organization, whereas *climate* refers to perceptions of persons in the organization that reflect those norms, assumptions, and beliefs.

As a consequence, one can assess the climate of any school with several instruments (Halpin and Croft 1963), including the Organizational Climate Index (Steinhoff 1965). Within organizations, parts may develop their own subculture and climate. Kindergarten teachers, for example, may have tons of stuff all over the place, while upper grades may not have as many manipulatives in every nook and cranny. Kindergarten kiddies usually have a milk-and-cookies break at mid-morning and naps in the afternoon, but not the fifth grade. Few banks have a cookies-and-milk mid-morning break and fewer have afternoon naps. Kindergarten kids usually have a recess, a dying practice for the upper grades in many schools today.

### Reflective Questions

1. *What different subcultures have developed in your school?*
2. *District, elementary schools?*
3. *How did they come about?*

## Can the Principal (and Teacher) Create a Positive Subculture and Climate? If So, How?

It's a key—and vital—question to ask: What is the role of the principal in creating a subculture? For most of us, this may be a somewhat startling question, but it gets to the heart of being an effective leader. Some leaders (and teachers, who are, of course, leaders in their classrooms and in other settings) take the role of the hapless Charlie Brown, standing around and being a passive observer as the norms and subcultures form. (Actually, Charlie helps them form, as Lucy and others observe sarcastically.) Others may recognize that their role is to be more assertive. But we have to be clear that norms and subcultures are created in all groups as we interact with each other. Just because we do not recognize that they are forming does not mean that they are not coalescing around us. The big problem is that many of us usually are quite unaware as they develop around us, until they hit us like a two-by-four.

This is certainly true in families, in classes, in schools, in the military, in stores. Whenever you have organizations, a subculture is created. Unfortunately, most of us really do not focus on this process, often until we belatedly recognize that some behavior patterns we do not like have mushroomed and slammed into our lives.

The leader, then, has to be very aware not only of the developing culture, but also the norms he or she wants to build. What would you like your school, or class, or school district to look like?

- people generally happy and supportive, developing trust for each other
- people being creative
- taking risks to do good work
- working cooperatively and supporting each other
- all people liking each other (or at least able to work with each other) and kids
- being able to deal with inevitable conflict
- using difference of opinions and conflict to improve things (how do we grow without conflict?)
- people working really hard, but smartly

*Reflective Questions*

1. *What other behaviors would you like to see in your schools?*
2. *And, if these become some of your goals, what can you do to pull them off?*

A good deal of the rest of this book will deal with these questions—and more, for example, dealing with what a constructivist principal does and how he or she behaves in the complex world called school these days.

# SUMMARY

In this part, we dealt with organizations, which we noted are man-made entities. We construct them, so that sociologists consider them as socially constructed, shared realities. We focused primarily on how organizations develop structure in their need to continue their viability. We generalized that organizations create positions and roles as the building blocks, the structure, of their existence. We noted that roles are expressed by role expectations, which can differ a great deal, so that our perceptions of a number of different interpretations can direct how we perform our roles.

Thus, we can generate a good deal of conflict as our role expectations develop. We found that we can have conflicting expectations for acting out one role and that different reference groups often have divergent expectations regarding how our roles should be played out. Even within reference groups or social systems, role expectations may conflict. We suggested that Guba and Getzels's model helped clarify sources of role conflict.

We also dug into two other components of structure, hierarchy and authority. We discovered the depth of Barnard's contribution to understanding authority with his formulation that for it to be accepted, four conditions were necessary. Thus, our contemporary grasp of authority presently is that it rests on communication—and its acceptance by subordinates, not on its delegation from higher levels.

Last, we focused on another key component of structure, the social system, which leads to the norms (read, customs) created by people interacting in social systems and organizations and resulting subcultures and climates that emerge. We noted that the social system is a key idea in understanding how organizations work. Not only are families social systems, but also subgroups, which are social systems that inevitably form in all organizations, including friendship and work groups. Inevitably, we develop customs or norms in all our social systems, which develop into patterns which become the subculture of the organization. And, we noted that we can create positive supportive subcultures if we become aware of the processes that generate subcultures. We will point to those processes as part of a case study or two.

# GLOSSARY

**authority**   develops when subordinates accept your communications as coming from a source vested with the right to make decisions—see chapter 8.

**climate**   perceptions of people in an organization that reflect its norms, assumptions, beliefs.

**culture**   shared, learned behavior, assumptions, and beliefs that people in a society develop in connection with social living.

**custom**   a practice or behavior people in a group normally do; driving on the right.

**hierarchy**   the structure of an organization, its levels.

**idiographic dimension**   the individual's personality and needs, need dispositions.

**nomothetic dimension**   roles and role expectations developed in an organization.

**norm**   a custom or practice of a group of people or culture.

**organization**   a formal body that has been organized or made into an organized whole.

**position**   various jobs or statuses in an organization, such as student, teacher, principal.

**reference group**   a group of people regarded as prestigious.

**role**   the dynamic enactment of a position; a series of expectations defining the role.

**role conflict**   occurs when expectations for a role are perceived to differ.

**role expectations**   various expectations different reference groups develop for a role.

**social system**   any two or more people in a meaningful relationship.

**structure**   the internal organization of an organization.

**subculture**   the mini-culture that people in parts of a culture develop, such as in an organization.

*Chapter Five*

# Hidden Behaviors That Make Organizations (Read, Schools) Tick

## Images, Cycles, and Pulls—Revealed

The behavior of an organization often can be predicted by assuming it to be controlled by a cabal of its enemies.

—Robert Conquest's Law

*Reflective Question*

*Do you want to be able to describe, analyze, and predict accurately what your leaders and those in other organizations are going to do?*

The models we're describing offer powerful predictors of both short- and long-range behavior of those in leadership positions—enabling each of us to predict how our organizations are going to become, so we can control our own professional lives. So, read on.

Our last chapter, on what makes organizations tick, dealt with developing structure such as *positions*, *then roles* and *role expectations*, which can lead to *role conflict*, then *hierarchy* and *authority*, which Barnard noted was based on communications. The chapter's next section, Universal Elements: Social Systems, zeroed in on social systems (read, groups) that form universal informal structures within the formal structure of the organization. We found that the formal and informal organizations inevitably develop a *culture* and numerous *subcultures*, and suggested that we can improve our lives in our schools by creating subcultures we want. Of course, we can only do that if we know what we're doing. (Incidentally, not knowing what we're doing can lead to our undoing.)

This chapter digs away at some key trends and patterns that inevitably occur, but which are generally so gradual and unobtrusive that they often slip by us, leaving most of us blissfully unaware of them. The first section consists of analyzing *metaphors* or *images* about organizations that we may believe and accept unthinkingly. Next, we deal with *long-term cycles* that formal organizations inevitably cycle through, described, analyzed, and predicted by the **Tri-Partite Theory of Organizational Succession and Control** (1969, 2000), which impacts their productivity to the point that they lose their way. In the physical world, we call this **entropy**, that is, energy systems (certainly what organizations such as schools obviously are) lose their energy—often for very, very long periods. The third smaller chunk of the chapter consists of *pulls* that various levels of social systems within organizations inevitably develop that seem so irrational—until we grasp the dynamics of the pulls—and then they make clear sense, explaining all kinds of behavior that may puzzle and even exasperate us tremendously.

## IMAGES (OR METAPHORS) OF ORGANIZATIONS

*Reflective Question*

*Why are we talking about images of organizations?*

Many images we use are so commonplace that often we simply are not only unaware of them in our thinking, we also do not even consider them as guiding our behavior. Often, these are **assumptions**, but we do not even recognize our beliefs as assumptions. For example, Americans think that we are the greatest country in the world. We're shocked when other cultures criticize us. Oddly, virtually every country and culture believes they are the best. It's **ethnocentrism**, the belief that your group or culture is superior. Almost all cultures believe that.

Other assumptions? These days, we assume that we will have problems with any bureaucracy (despite the fact that they were developed to help smooth our interactions). Next, we assume that people believe the way *we* do (called solipsism)—and, are somewhat surprised when we find that lots of people believe differently than we do, often much differently.

*Reflective Question*

*How does this play out in our thinking about and dealing with organizations?*

People have been thinking about organizations for as long as they've been around. And, we tend to use symbols to describe our organizations. As we go through these various approaches, we might keep in mind the story of blind men describing the elephant. Each had a piece of the truth, but no one had an overall view.

Using Morgan's (1997) insights in part, we'll look at *images or metaphors*, which treat our organizations as:

* a machine;
* an organism;
* a culture;
* a political system;
* a self-learning system — that is, a learning organization;
* a family;
* involved in change;
* an instrument of domination — or, a psychic prison (you know, a bad marriage);
* a **social sorting** mechanism; and
* a refuge.

## The Organization (Read, School) as a Machine

This is too easy. Most of us, when thinking about a machine, think of a clock; lots of people actually compared organizations to clocks or other machines. This is essentially behind Frederick Taylor's (1911) construction of scientific management. Most of us think that this is dead, gone, like the dodo. Is it?

Here's how McDonald's, Wal-Mart, and a host of other industries have implemented Taylor's ideas into workplace routines. His ideas are simple. He even told workers, "You're not supposed to think. There are other people paid for thinking around here." Workers were no more literally than a pair of hands to do what they were told to do. Taylor simplified jobs so that workers would be:

* cheap;
* easy to train;
* easy to supervise;
* easy to replace; and
* easy to standardize.

Note how Taylor's five simple principles stick like glue to the fast food industry:

1. Shift all responsibility for the organization of work from the worker to the manager. Managers should do all the thinking relating to the planning and design of work, leaving workers with the task of implementation.
2. Use scientific methods to determine the most efficient way of doing work. Design the worker's task accordingly, specifying the precise way in which the work is to be done.
3. Select the best person to perform the job.
4. Train the worker to do the job efficiently.
5. Monitor work performance to ensure that appropriate work procedures are followed and that appropriate results are achieved (Morgan 1997, 23).

Taylor developed the notion of paying people by the amount of work they produced—piecework. At Wal-Mart and other super marts, clerks who scan are evaluated by the number and speed of items they scan. Insurance companies regularly fire clerks on Friday who do not meet quotas.

Notice how many state governments have adopted Taylorism with their state testing programs in treating teachers and principals. If their classes and schools don't ratchet up scores (usually reading, writing, and math), regardless of socioeconomics, they are replaced like widgets on an assembly line. So, many in charge of states and the nation have bought into Taylor's scientific management ideas that labor (read, teachers and principals) should be cheap, easy to train, easy to supervise, easy to replace, and easy to standardize (like factory workers). So, in today's teacher shortages, we hire people with a degree in any area, give them a short injection, and expect them to be able to teach professionally (even reading) (Catalanecco 2005, 1).

The fast food industry has McDonaldized, since they're dealing with cheap, temporary, easy-to-train workers. But, can kids be standardized like hamburgers? Teachers? Principals? As we saw in chapter 3, What Makes Terry Tick?, we are all individuals, with huge differences in personalities, talents, interests. So, perceiving schools as machines collapses. We are never going to be all standardized Lake Woebegoners, where every kid is above average academically.

## The Organization (School) as an Organism

At the opposite continuum of considering schools and other organizations as mechanical is that they are organisms. Engineers experimenting to increase production at the wire relay room at Hawthorne's Western Electric plant in Cicero, Illinois, actually thought that the world was a clock, and people, naturally, would react to stimuli like mechanical devices.

So, they experimented by increasing light, then more rest periods, then longer lunches. The women responded by increasing production at each new benefit. Then engineers reduced these conditions, until light in the relay room was as bright as a full moon. But the women kept increasing production. The concrete sequential engineers, treating women as machines, were confounded.

Frustrated, management brought in social scientist Elton Mayo to figure this out. Mayo *talked* to the women, discovering that they felt special, because they were the focus of so much attention. Eureka! The "Hawthorne Effect" was born.

The problem with this metaphor is that an organism *actually is* a physical, living entity. While schools can be perceived as organisms, they are not physical, living beings; they are human constructs. And while natural selection can drive physical organisms extinct, schools and human organizations can become flexible, and can adapt to major environmental changes. While this image points out the fallacy of considering schools as machines, treating schools literally as organisms is not quite accurate either.

## The Organization (School) as a Culture

If you read chapter 4, on what makes organizations tick, you might think it my viewpoint. The culture metaphor provides keen insights into how schools operate. Almost every aspect of school life has symbolic significance (visits to the principal's office, homecoming rituals, elementary school carnivals, volunteer tutors, bells). The image points clearly to our shared and complex systems of meaning (about which administrators hired from business or military usually have no clue, and often fail because of this lack).

Organizations essentially are *created*, *socially constructed*, *shared realities*. Therefore, if we're sharp enough, we can create some customs and symbols. Certainly, organizations do develop a culture (shared language, symbols, beliefs, norms that people develop as we interact), which is crucial to understand in working with them. That's why new administrators, who race into action too early without finding out the culture, often self-destruct. But organizations are considerably more than a culture. They are also political systems (and a lot more).

## Schools as Political Systems

Pretty clearly, anyone looking at organizations, including schools, discovers that some people have more power, more prestige, more influence than others. And some social systems have more of these "goodies" than others. We can look at the power and influence of various social systems as similar to those fraternities and sororities that make their way to the top of the pecking order, grabbing the lion's share of homecoming kings and queens, while others get shut out and, unhappily, feel deprived.

In actuality, political systems are arenas for conflicting interests and power, as well as for accommodation and decision making. But, again, schools are far more than mere battlefields for grabbing more power, even though schools (and organizations) are systems for governance. The preceding chapter addressed Barnard's fundamental approach of looking at authority as a communication that causes it to be accepted by a subordinate. In this thinking, the principal's authority and power rests upon the *teachers' accepting* it, a somewhat sobering approach. If principals violate enough major norms, they may destroy their authority and create a rebellion, often without actually recognizing it. Have you ever experienced such an event?

Another interesting aspect of schools as political systems is to review how conflict is managed. Usually, in elementary schools, teachers do not like to confront anyone, so resentments can simmer. I've found that a session or two on conflict management can reduce this to manageable levels. Too much emphasis on schools as political systems can encourage some into excessive power struggles, which turns schools into battlefields, a disastrous outcome.

## Schools as a Family

My clever wife, reading a table of contents of a book on organizational metaphors, noted that the image of the family was missing. So, here goes.

This metaphor seems useful in describing some schools, usually smaller, and not departmentalized. You can develop a good big school, but it's much harder to pull that off (S. Leggett, personal communication, 1995). And the actual physical distance in space from each other in the faculty that large size generates also becomes **social distance**. People begin saying, "You fourth grade teachers in that wing," or, "I simply never get to talk to the English guys now that I'm so far from their turf."

One solution Dr. Leggett proposed is to set up office space mixing people from different departments, so they get to know each other and communicate face-to-face, a somewhat radical proposal, but one that works. Another is to decentralize into smaller units, called halls, houses, or small learning communities (SLCs). That can ensure familyhood, but the issue of relating to other units arises. I shoot for decentralizing into smaller units and work out ways for each unit to relate to each other. Recently, students on a planning task force suggested having a representative from each SLC on the planning group of other SLCs to establish formal and informal communication to improve relationships and coordination. Anyway, the idea of a family is a neat one, but size becomes an unfriendly factor in pulling this off.

Another negative can occur when a Theory X principal is appointed to a school that works as a family or team. Often, teams start dissolving. One indication of trouble in a smoothly running school is when key people and social systems bail. It's a symptom of **Gresham's Law** applied to organizations. Gresham, a couple of centuries ago, concluded that when countries begin to debase their gold and silver coins with cheaper metals, people catch on, and hoard good money. He concluded that bad money drives out good. Similarly, when authoritarian administrators follow those who have facilitated development of family feelings, good people are driven out. Wise leadership might become aware of this principle in evaluating competence.

## The School as a Self-Learning System, a Learning Organization

Some literature has sprung up touting schools as learning organizations (Senge 1990; Sullivan and Glanz 2006). While some success has occurred, this is not an easy row to hoe. Some research has begun to indicate that this can, indeed, occur, but the metaphor blurs the essential truth that individuals and social systems construct social realities in organizations, and they can readily go awry when conditions change. Anyway, usually we learn in spurts. We can hardly expect our organizations to do otherwise. However, this can be a fruitful way to work. It's a sort of internal self-improvement plan, not easy to pull off, but rewarding. Obviously, it requires a planning structure (Isaacson 2004).

As an assistant superintendent and then superintendent, we instituted a curriculum steering committee structure to generate curriculum into the system *as a routine* with huge involvement, a structure which still operates. (See chapter 6 for the structure and rules.) The next major section, the Tri-Partite Theory of Succession and Control, addresses this.


## ORGANIZATIONS AS CHANGE

*Reflective Question*

*What do you feel when you hear the word "change"?*


This image of the organization is a tough one. Most of us want stability in some part of our lives. So, if our personal lives are unstable, and our professional lives become that way, it can be pretty hard to take. As a consequence, many of us (especially the concrete sequential personalities) really aren't too thrilled when schools start making major changes. But, let's twist the way we look at change by perceiving that *change represents opportunity.* Any change can be perceived as providing opportunities to accomplish key goals that were difficult when the school or system was stable. This is why some of us perceive change—any change—as providing opportunities to accomplish priorities. As soon as I realized that, I looked for any change on the horizon to provide openings.

That takes planning, and *a system for developing controlled change*, such as the curriculum steering committee structure presented in the next chapter, chapter 6. Chapters 9 and 10 provide an example of a principal who moved her school into a constructivist model when opportunity arose. She even did her doctoral dissertation on the resulting case study (Isaacson 2004).

# ORGANIZATIONS AS CONTROLLING, EVEN DOMINATING—AS PSYCHIC PRISONS (LIKE SOME BAD MARRIAGES AND JOBS)

*Reflective Question*

*Can we become prisoners of our metaphors, our beliefs?*

We can—if we believe the ideas, assumptions, and images of our organizations so strongly that we become blind to alternative images and ideas, thus failing even to perceive and to deal with looming changes. A sad, but arresting example is that often those in toxic marriages with physical abuse fear leaving the system. The organization (marriage) has become a psychic prison. When I asked a class last week if anyone had been divorced and several people raised their hands, I then asked if any of their former marriages were psychic prisons. The point was made in a classroom as silent as a tomb.

Illustrations abound in industry and business. The honchos at IBM believed strongly that its mainframe would continue to serve the world, but the PC came along, causing its fortunes to slide. American auto manufacturers endured the same agony in their certainty that big, gas-guzzling cars were the way to go—even when the 1973 OPEC crisis overtook us, even when the Japanese, then the European, then the Korean car companies began to overtake them—and actually did. American companies were slow to recognize the huge market changes crashing down, slowly eroding their market share. Yet, Ford unveiled the Edsel just before this period. Deming himself noted that management was responsible for 85 percent of all quality problems (March 1986). These organizations could not break out of their mental boxes.

Unfortunately, a number of people, some in very influential political and economic positions, want to diminish if not destroy public schools, as Bracey wrote in *The War Against the Public Schools* (2002). Hopefully, we've awakened and are taking steps to improve schools, particularly those in inner-city environments. Similarly, we find the testing movement has gone from an idea to a movement to a madness, to a craze, to a mania. As a consequence we test every year, delighting the testing corporations' CEOs.

In Florida, in 2003, forty-three thousand third graders did not pass the writing exam and were in danger of failing; twelve thousand seniors were in danger of not graduating, all because of a single test. Even such drastic outcomes did not deter the political powers from writing into law that if third graders did not pass writing tests a second time, they would be failed again. Actually, about a quarter did make it, but most did not. Consequently, many kids are eleven years old in fourth grade, two years older than their peers.

We find principals and teachers, some of whom are warm, supporting people, making lists of elementary kids to be held back, despite the devastation this creates. If kids are failed once, research reveals that about two-thirds will not graduate. If a kid is failed twice, over 95 percent drop out, so with testing pressures afflicting us, our dropout rate is climbing, not quite what Goals 2000 wanted. Doesn't this make schools psychic prisons? As soon as these kids hit sixteen, they're out. As adults, how do you think they're going to feel about supporting schools' requests for rate increases?

## Schools as Social Sorting Mechanisms

Many people inside and outside of our schools are still sublimely unaware that schools reflect, support, and sustain socioeconomic structures, that kids who are upper-middle and upper class get better grades, flood gifted classes, fill band slots considerably more, and dominate National Honor Societies. Schools essentially send a rather clear message not lost on faculty and students. The vehicle by which this is carried out is ability grouping and tracking (Oakes 1985; Shapiro, Benjamin, and Hunt 1995; Brantlinger 1995).

People treated this way feel humiliated, not knowing what to do about it. In my university classes, when we deal with ability grouping, I always ask if someone has been grouped into lower ability classes. Always several respond. Once, a young woman said she had—and burst into tears. The class was silent as a tomb. Another teacher in his upper thirties said he had, but he'd recovered. His friends assured me that he was still devastated twenty years later.

The horrendous aspect of this practice is that the kids *actually believe* they are below average, not an outcome of which we can point to with pride as a momentous educational achievement. As noted in chapter 3, people are bundles of a considerable variety of talents (planning, creative, human relations, decision making, physical, organizing, communicating, etc.). Academic talents are merely one set. Taylor (1968), noted that most people are above average in at least one talent. Convincing kids that they are below average falsifies reality, doing a life-changing disservice.

## School as a Refuge, a Safe Haven

While this image might surprise some, for many children school is, indeed, a haven. For many kids who are hungry, breakfasts and lunch may be the only regular meals they get—period. One young woman, who co-taught with me, indicated that after school, every day she and her brother would go off to scavenge for food in dumpsters, since they had none at home. In some states, 20 percent or more of our kids are in poverty, and many are hungry, as well.

For many kids, chaotic conditions at home may make schools havens, settings of psychological safety. Some kids may find role models there, others mentors. Unfortunately the testing mania is making school a gauntlet for far too many kids, teachers, and administrators.

## PREDICTING CYCLES IN ORGANIZATIONS: THE TRI-PARTITE THEORY OF ORGANIZATIONAL SUCCESSION AND CONTROL

Most of us tend to analyze organizations for relatively short time periods of months or a year or two. A longer focus provides important insights (and, an ability to predict accurately) the *phases* organizations, including schools, pass through in their *careers*. We know that men and women pass through stages as we chug through our lives. Researchers (Sheehy 1976; Levinson 1978) discovered that we develop a career as we pass through our life's phases. These insights have found their way into pop culture (middle-age crazies for men, breaking loose for women).

*What if organizations develop phases in their careers*, but over a relatively long time? The Tri-Partite Theory states that they do (Wilson, Byar, Shapiro, and Schell 1969; Shapiro, Benjamin, and Hunt 1995). This theory

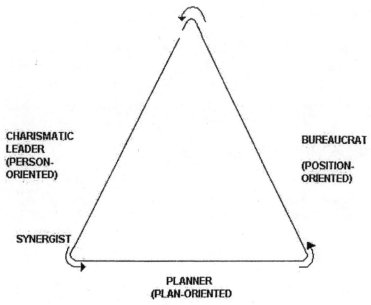

**Figure 5.1.  Phases of Organizational Change: Tri-Partite Theory**

states that organizations, like physical systems, are *entropic*. That is, we know that all energy systems in the physical world eventually lose their energy, run downhill. Cars do, clocks do, so do solar systems. Do human systems? This theory states that human organizations, schools, companies, corporations, also lose their energy, eventually running downhill (see figure 5.1).

*Reflective Questions*

1. *Why are so many of our organizations (surely that includes schools) seemingly stuck in the mud, so resistant to change for so long?*
2. *We know that each of us (men and women) go through phases in our lives. Have you ever thought that schools, organizations, have a career, a series of phases through which they pass?*
3. *Have you ever been in a school that seems mired in red tape, where rules and regulations simply dominate?*
4. *Or, have you ever been in a school or district where exciting things were happening—and, in which you had fun?*

Everyone can describe organizations seemingly dominated by red tape, rules, regulations. The school or district can be described best as bureaucratically dominated, with the principal or superintendent more of a caretaker, maintaining order, more a tinkerer than a developer. Essentially, nothing happens, routine dominates. Its mission has been forgotten, with people looking back to a mythical golden age when it was exciting to live in it. People at the top are careful to follow the rules to protect themselves, are fearful of making changes, so the place is locked into routine, status quo, stagnation. Dozens of organizations illustrate this, from Chrysler before Iacocca (needing a federal bailout to survive) to IBM, who thought mainframes would dominate the world, to General Motors (which had a 50 percent share of the auto market once to its well-under 25 percent today), to many state departments, local schools, and districts locked into the status quo.

## The Charismatic Leader: The Person-Oriented Phase of the Organization's Career

At some point, the board of directors, or board of education, or chief executive becomes seriously concerned that disaster is looming for the total organization or school (three straight years of failing state tests). They begin to look for a dynamic individual with vision, energy, ideas, charisma to break the school out of its funk and reenergize it. Such a *charismatic* person energizes people. People come out of the woodwork, attracted by her vision and energy. She brings hope for the future, generating loyalty to herself. This state of an organization's career we call *person-orientation*. The leader? The *charismatic*.

Examples? Mahatma and Indira Gandhi in India; John Fitzgerald Kennedy, Michael Jordan, generals Norman Schwarzkopf, Robert E. Lee, Dwight D. Eisenhower, and George S. Patton; and Illinois senator Barack Obama. In education, John Dewey; Robert Maynard Hutchins, president of the University of Chicago and champion of the Great Books; Al Shanker, former president of the American Federation of Teachers, come to mind. So does Martin Luther King.

The charismatic leader's role is fascinating, since he/she breaks the organization out of its doldrums, its mind-numbing routines, by expressing with ideas the hopes, aspirations, and interests of doing significant things professionally and personally. Such a person excites the imagination of large numbers of people and can lead them to exciting ventures. Such leadership facilitates generating large numbers of initiatives, usually uncoordinated, to which many flock. People express a great deal of hope since the future is wide open in comparison with the scenario painted above. People actually like being there.

Actions tend to be short-range, exciting, with people developing hosts of ideas, initiatives, plans, often uncoordinated. In this person-oriented phase of its career, the organization is at its most dynamic. Unfortunately, when asked if people have lived in such a phase, usually less than one-third respond.

## The Planner and Plan-Orientation: The Planning Phase

Usually, the person-oriented phase of an organization's career tends to be short—two to four years. People begin to tire of the action, want more stability. The charismatic may get attracted to another organization that wants the pizzazz and publicity he/she generates, or gets shot out of the saddle, leaving followers anxious to retain some ideas. So, they try to recruit someone who can take the later ideas and fashion them into a plan. So, the organization generally unwittingly selects a *planner* to head up the next phase of its career.

*Reflective Questions*

1. *Have you ever worked in a school or district that was headed by a planner?*
2. *How did he/she operate? Was he/she as charismatic as the former leader?*

Obviously, planners come in different shapes and sizes ranging from someone who focuses on one idea (block scheduling, improved report cards) to those who advocate system-wide and systemic change (decentralization into small learning communities, or middle schools, or continuous progress, full-service schools, constructivist teaching). Examples of planners are not as evident as charismatic leaders, since most planners tend to work behind the scenes and do not exhibit as much charisma. Dou-

glas MacArthur was a planner, as were Omar Bradley, Bill Gates, Lee Iacocca, and Donald Trump. Martin Luther King and the two Gandhis
should be mentioned. We have more difficulty in citing planners in education. Dale Parnell, the founder of the Tech-Prep movement in community colleges, is one example. Whom do *you* nominate?

Plans can range from simple (changing the report card) to complex, such
as decentralizing by converting a school into SLCs, moving into a middle
school, restructuring the district (three- or four-year high school), developing portfolios, etc. So, plans can range from short-range, small to comprehensive and long-term. Moving into team and/or constructivist teaching
represents a multiyear endeavor.

The plan guides and harnesses the organization's energies, focus, resources. In comparison with the person-oriented view of the future, which
is wide open, plan orientation focuses on achieving the plan. Action is
long-range in comparison with the person-oriented phase, which can result in people becoming loyal to the plan, contrasting with the person-oriented phase where loyalty is to the leader.

*Reflective Questions*

1. *Have you ever been in an organization dominated by a plan?*
2. *What was it like? How were priorities set?*
3. *How long did it last? (key question)*

## The Fate of Plans and the Planning Phase

Most plans follow an inevitable, fixed, and fateful career or template—
unless one knows the pattern. And, therein lies its Achilles' heel. Usually,
a plan garners a good deal of support if involvement is heavy and a minority doesn't force it upon an acquiescent majority.

However, as time passes, the day-to-day, bit-by-bit incremental nature
of decision making focusing on immediate crises and conditions tends to
drift slowly away from holding the plan aloft as a prism guiding all action
and resources. As time unfolds, new people enter who have not participated in its development and implementation, and so are not necessarily
passionate advocates, while the original pioneers leave. The new give lip
service to the plan, but usually feel less loyalty.

After two or three years, the plan begins to be honored more in the breach than in actually guiding actions. By five years, the plan has slid out of our consciousness and gets brought up by old timers reminiscing about the good old days. As an example, I was once hired by a prominent Midwestern university lab school to be a field work supervisor and core teacher, teaching language arts and social studies in the seventh grade in a brand new building built for that purpose. Oddly, I returned eight years later to interview for the small city's assistant superintendency; so of course, I looked up my old friends. By this time, my colleagues and I had developed the Tri-Partite Theory. I did not ask the naïve question, "What happened to Core?" Instead, I asked predictively, "Hey, guys, when did Core die?" to a taken-aback group. No one answered at first—no one knew. Core had simply slipped away; people had a difficult time pinning down when it had stopped.

More organizational dynamics explain these change processes. As people in organizations develop their plans, they set up rules and regulations to achieve their goals. They begin to establish carefully crafted job descriptions, designed for the same purpose. So, red tape flourishes and begins to rule the roost, with secretaries even telling top administrators what to do and what they cannot do. So, slowly, spontaneity, creativity, vigor, gets squeezed out.

In this process, the plan begins to lose its vision on people's imagination and day-to-day actions. Priorities change, and by this time the planner, like the charismatic leader, a nomad, looks around for new challenges. Or she has left for a school looking for a plan.

### The Bureaucrat: The Position-Oriented
### Phase of the Organization's Career

By this time the planner has been succeeded by a person whose main focus is to stabilize—in short, a bureaucrat who generally likes red tape and regulations, often to increase his/her power. The great upswing of hope generated in the person-oriented phase has long disappeared, since the organization tends to become backward-looking, pointing to past glories and achievements. The leader tends to be a stabilizer, or a tinkerer, who has problems breaking out of the box. He/she becomes a prisoner of the box—or, creates the box in which to feel safe.

When crises occur, the organization shudders and copes with symptoms, rather than on long-range creative solutions. Often such an administrator will be authoritarian, focusing on control, a Theory X person. Thus, people, at best loyal to the position, are *position oriented*.

Many ask how long various phases last. Unfortunately, this is the longest, since often the superiors will hire someone who does not want to, or cannot, rock the boat. Most organizations seem to reside in this phase, often for a long time. If a school or district hires an insider, they're usually going to stay in the bureaucratic phase, since they're looking for stability.

## The Synergist

Once in a blue moon, we can find someone who is both charismatic *and* a planner, a **synergist**. You might note that several are repeated, including General MacArthur, Robert E. Lee, Iacocca, Robert Maynard Hutchins, Dale Parnell. Obviously, Mahatma Gandhi fits, as does Martin Luther King. Whom do you nominate?

Synergists are exceedingly useful in breaking out of doldrums in which a position-oriented school or district finds itself. This rarity combines both charisma *and* planning, so we have a real package. Since they are rare, synergistic staffing is a possibility, with a charismatic leader and a planner (providing they can work together). They have to be mature enough to deal with jealousy that can arise when one receives more kudos. Both are essential. Obviously, examples of this arise when teams have coaches exemplifying these talents, as with the Chicago Bears of the early 1980s when Mike Ditka was the head coach and Buddy Ryan handled the famous "46" defense.

How to beat this entropy? Better replan every two to three years, or the plan will be lost.

## PREDICTING PULLS FOR POWER AND CONTROL FROM DIFFERENT PARTS OF ORGANIZATIONS

*Reflective Question*

*Did you ever wish you'd written a particular book?*

I have. It's *The Structuring of Organizations* by Henry Mintzberg (1979). Mintzberg developed a logo delineating five different parts of the organization (see figure 5.2).

The first is the **strategic apex** (the lads and ladies in control). The **middle line** consists of middle management (principals and their assistants). The **operating core** consists of peons who do the work (teachers, aides, etc.). Two more groups people the organization: the **technostructure**, consisting of technocrats, such as computer people and other analysts, and **support staff**, including office, cafeteria, and custodial personnel.

My reason for pulling Mintzberg into this chapter is simple. He points to each social system as exerting a different "pull" on the organization because of its interests (see figure 5.3).

Predicting these pulls can make you seem like a genius—because you will be miles ahead of everyone in predicting the actions of each organization's parts. So, here goes.

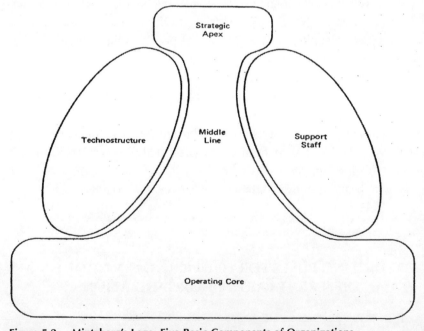

**Figure 5.2.   Mintzberg's Logo: Five Basic Components of Organizations**
*Source:* Henry Mintzberg, *Structuring of Organizations,* 1st ed. © 1979, p. 20. Reprinted by permission of Pearson Education, Inc., Upper Saddle River, NJ.

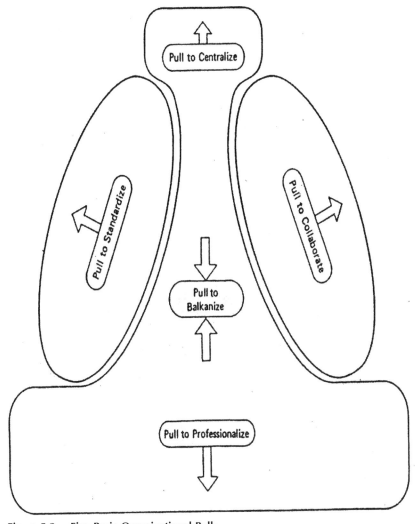

**Figure 5.3.   Five Basic Organizational Pulls**
*Source:* Henry Mintzberg, *Structuring of Organizations*, 1st ed. © 1979, p. 302. Reprinted by permission of Pearson Education, Inc., Upper Saddle River, NJ.

What do you think the strategic apex want to do? Of course, their chief concern is *controlling decision making*, so they pull to *centralize all* decisions, to control everything. Is this true of your strategic apex?

How about the middle line? They want *autonomy* to do whatever they want to. So, they try to draw power from the strategic apex. Thus, they want to *balkanize* the organization. That is, they want to be autonomous (like the Balkan nations split into numerous little countries [Slovenia, Serbia, Kosevo, Macedonia]), so they can control their own shops and make their own decisions.

How about the operating core? They want decentralization also, but their pull is to *professionalize*. Teacher literature for decades reflects our desire for increasing professionalization. The National Board of Professional Teacher Standards' increasing popularity attests to this drive. Similarly, in hospitals, this has been the focus of nurses in becoming professionally prestigious nurse-practitioners. This way, they build prestige and power, partly countering that of physicians.

The technostructure? They want to *standardize* work processes, such as all computers be IBM or IBM clones, or Apples. Central office people in larger districts want all schools to use the same computer system to schedule, or to use the same report card system. Thus, these folks want to standardize work processes.

And support staff? According to Mintzberg, they gain the most influence when, because of their expertise, *we need them to collaborate* with us. When they're out sick, almost nothing gets done. Our work place gets gummed up (since we're stuck without them).

I find these pulls fascinating, because we can predict fairly well what each component of the organization's interests are, what their likely strategic stance will be for many issues. Take report cards. The technostructure, to simplify their lives, try to make all alike, lobbying for that end. In one nearby district, the techies lobbied for a common middle school report card to simplify their lives—and, actually were successful.

## Reflective Questions

1. *What do you think principals (the middle line) want?*
2. *Do all elementary schools want the same report card?*
3. *Should all schools, small learning communities (SLCs), or halls be the same?*
4. *If a school moves toward a particular organization, will it be hamstrung if required to have the same report card?*
5. *What about discipline?*

Many teachers in the operating core would love to be able to throw a kid out without having to have principal approval. Actually, such legislation gets considered once in a while. But, interesting problems occur if this is tried. How about enrollment? A principal in a district I once worked in actually said that she would not admit any more kids. Can a district permit this autonomy?

The concept of pulls, like many of the ideas and processes described in this book, has considerable value as a tool for us to describe, analyze, and predict and then to deal more effectively with our schools.

## SUMMARY

In this chapter, the second part on what makes organizations tick, we dealt at some length with a number of key images and metaphors that often control our thinking, and, therefore, our lives in our organizations. We tried to breathe life into them so that we can be more objective in deciding which, if any, we want to use.

We took a quick overview of the phases of the cycle that organizations (including schools) inevitably career through, the Tri-Partite Theory of Organizational Succession and Control. We also took a brief look at the pulls the five parts of the organization exert in their desire to achieve their perceptions of their purposes.

Thus, chapter 5 presents some useful tools for us to analyze and predict to control our professional lives, in the process providing the possibility of creating more personal and professional satisfaction.

## GLOSSARY

**assumptions**   starting points in everyone's thinking.

**entropy**   a theory that organizations, like physical entities, experience loss of energy, purpose.

**ethnocentrism**   the belief in a culture that its practices are superior.

**Gresham's Law**   the theory that when governments debase their coinage, people hoard good coins.

**middle line**   midlevel administrators (principals, managers).

**operating core**   the workers (peons) in organizations.

**social distance**   the space that people in various groups feel separated from each other.

**social sorting**   the process in schools of rewarding and separating the social classes.

**strategic apex**   those who run our organization.

**support staff**   clerical, office folks.

**synergist**   a leader who combines charisma with planning talent; a relative rarity.

**technostructure**   the geeks in organizations.

**Tri-Partite Theory of Organizational Succession and Control**   a theory that organizations cycle through a career of three phases with four associated leadership styles: charismatic, planner, synergist, bureaucrat.

## Chapter Six

# But First, We Need a Purpose

## A Case Study

A purpose is the eternal condition of success.

—Theodore T. Munger

High performing leaders understand that the "seals" and "gaskets" that hold an organization together is *commitment*.

—Emmett C. Murphy and Mark A. Murphy,
*Leading on the Edge of Chaos*

### SO, WHY A PURPOSE?

*Reflective Questions*

1. *We'll answer a question with a question: How do you know where to head without a purpose?*
2. *A second (humorous?) question: How do you know you're there when you get there?*

A little personal experience to make the point: I moved to a somewhat larger, some thought more prestigious, suburban district on the East Coast from a Midwestern independent city system which had developed a clear purpose and a well-thought-out *district-wide system for designing curriculum* to pull off the goals with massive teacher involvement. And it worked in spades.

We also designed a *pupil personnel system* for resolving each student's problems on a case-by-case basis. Because of this, all schools developed a variety of interesting programs carefully designed, competently implemented, and evaluated semiannually. The middle schools functioned with considerable flair (we picked a synergist [both a charismatic leader and a planner] as an assistant principal in one), and the high school also with its synergist principal moved into a modified **Trump model** (1959a; 1959b) with a hugely expanded program of studies (how about eighty-five courses each in social studies and English?).

The district I moved into as superintendent clearly had no central purpose driving it. People could identify which elementary school a kid attended, the junior high was a prison, and the high school wasn't doing anything significant, although a new high school was being built using the same organization. A couple of consultants coming through to fix the broken cafeteria program, run ineptly and losing tons of money, humorously commented that we had 385 independent schools (the number of faculty).

We had people with a variety of purposes, some even actually focused on education, most others on their own power aggrandizement or ego needs for recognition. The first third of every meeting was a struggle for power and control. And a lot of people, the board of education, and community members participated in the shenanigans. Essentially, we had anarchy!

Some board members interfered with administrative matters, people were hired for political favors, some supervisors were clearly incompetent, as were a couple of administrators (although that is not unusual). Too often, your political connections were the decision maker in getting something approved—or someone hired. The district had good, committed people, but they were not in position to turn it around. We needed to refocus the major norm of most decisions being made for political gain.

I cased the joint before taking the position, talking to teachers, administrators, kids, parents, community, street people in stores, bars, community centers, etc. Clearly, we needed to establish a small handful of clear purposes to which people could subscribe, which could be used to drive the district, rather than the scattered disorganization and self-focus.

## BARNARD'S THREE *INDISPENSABLE* ELEMENTS TO ORGANIZATIONS

### Common Purpose(s)

Leadership literature supports this. Chester Barnard, the father of modern administrative thinking, in his groundbreaking book, *The Functions of the Executive* (1938), stated *three indispensable* elements must operate for any organization to function effectively. The first is that the leader/administrator facilitates establishing common purposes. She does not establish them herself. The leader is focused on the necessity of people buying in, so cannot do the job alone.

### A Clear System of Communication

The next indispensable element is to establish a clear system of communication, so that purpose(s) can be communicated to everyone. That means *everyone*, since if we fail to communicate to every single person, the social systems who do not get the message will not believe it—nor will they become supportive. Barnard also established criteria for lines of communication—they should be direct and short.

### A System of Cooperation

The third indispensable element is to achieve a system of cooperation for people to achieve common purpose(s). If people do not want to cooperate, we cannot develop common purpose(s). This applies to organizations and, equally, to small, informal groups, even families. If kids or adults will not cooperate, what can be accomplished? We have an organization, but it is dysfunctional. It isn't working.

We need all three elements. A common purpose obviously cannot be achieved without a system of cooperation, which, in turn, is not achievable without a clear system of communication.


## THE CRUCIAL ROLE OF BUY-IN—IT GENERATES OWNERSHIP

The question is: How do we develop buy-in to a program? We do it by involving as many key social systems (see chapter 4) in and outside the organization in planning and implementation stages. If we do not pull this off, the payoff often is failure, or there are big problems in achieving goals. Usually, the program gets sloughed off in short order. If people are not involved, if programs are implemented over them, do they owe any loyalty to it? It's the folks in the organization who make it work.


## HOW TO PULL IT OFF: GENERATING BUY-IN—A PLANNING STRUCTURE AND PROCESS

The model I used to develop goals for a medium-sized district could be applied for any school. It was adapted from Wilson, Byar, Shapiro, and Schell's *Sociology of Supervision* (1969). If the school has twenty to twenty-five teachers, the entire staff should be involved on the Planning Committee, plus ethnic groups and the community. If the school is larger, representatives from all social systems, grades, ethnic groups, and the community should be involved. If the school is a middle grade or secondary school, students should certainly be involved, since that generates loyalty. Figure 6.1 illustrates the adapted model used to develop goals.

In the district, many people distrusted local institutions and organizations, tending to believe that anything they tried would not work and would collapse. As a consequence, we needed to reach leadership of key social systems, both of school and community—and we needed to move, we could not dawdle or people would lose interest.

The district, like many others, was essentially drifting, but quite anarchically in a position-oriented stage, using the Tri-Partite Theory (chapter

| July - Aug. 15 | Aug. 15 - Sept. 18 | Sept. 20 - Oct. 10 | Oct. 10 -15 | Oct. 15 - Nov. 1 |
| --- | --- | --- | --- | --- |
| STEP 1 | STEP 2 | STEP 3 | PRELIMINARY SUMMATION | STEP 4 |
| Establishment of the problem to be investigated to develop goals and directions for Long Beach City School District through involvement of staff, community, student body, and Board of Education. | Initiation of a structure for representative involvement of staff, community, student body, and Board of Education and deciding on what is and what is not the task[1]. Should also include university people if group feels need. | Small group meetings to challenge and evaluate existing programs and priorities. Recommendations of measurable behavioral objectives through involvement of staff, community, student body, and Board of Education. Continuous interchange (oral and written) among group members and those they represent[2]. | Total group meeting to compare, criticize and consolidate interim suggestions. Steering Committee pulls together suggestions into preliminary form. Everyone receives this. | Further small group meetings to consider additional or alternative goals. Evaluation of agreed upon goals. Continuous interchange with those represented. |

| Nov. 1 - 10 | Nov. 11 - Feb. 15 | March 1 | Summer | September |
| --- | --- | --- | --- | --- |
| STEP 5 | | | | |
| Total group meeting to formulate a comprehensive set of goals extrapolated from subgroups. | Lends itself now to an intelligent suggestion of materials, procedures, teachers, evaluations and consequently direction. Possible formation of recommending groups on implementing goals in each school and on establishing a curriculum-producing structure for the system. | Establishment of budget. | In-service workshops. Curriculum writing workshops. | Implementation of new structures, curriculum, procedures. |

[1] A task is to determine what we believe is good and right for learners.
[2] All notes of every meeting are to go to those represented.

Figue 6.1.  Preliminary Timetable

5). With this awareness, we were able to organize rapidly, so that by the end of July we could start the process of establishing meaningful goals.

We called a meeting of leaders of key social systems, including the teachers', principals', and noncertified unions, teachers from all levels of schools, teachers' aides, student councils, and informal representatives from all middle and high schools. We expanded beyond the normal community representatives from the parent-teacher associations (PTAs) to ensure that community agencies were involved, including key ethnic and racial group leaders.

## Beginnings

At the organizing meeting of fifty-five, people noted that the schools, which were considered pretty good in the past, were running downhill, that we needed to establish clear, practical common goals to operate efficiently and effectively. Because of considerable distrust, the normal operating procedure of a Planning Committee of eight to twelve or even fifteen people would not work, so we established a Planning Committee of twenty-four (eight students, eight parents and community, and eight administrators and teachers), plus three Working Committees of twenty-four members each. Step one was accomplished.

## Moving into Action

The large number of people, seventy-two, helped ease tensions and got a reasonably representative group. Each Working Committee published minutes to all members of every committee, the Planning Committee, the PTA, the board of education, all school personnel including all teachers, students, administrators, supervisors, aides, office, and noncertificated personnel, representatives of community centers, and key community organizations, including ethnic and racial groups. Minutes were translated into Spanish by a teacher.

At one time, a couple of colleagues suggested that I not participate in a meeting, since Working Committee members were unsure they could trust me not to influence their direction. So, I left, and when the next meeting was called, asked if they wanted me to participate, or not, and to chair the session, or not. They indicated that they wanted me to.

The Planning Committee met every two weeks to get minutes and feedback from all groups. We also agreed that we would make decisions as much as possible unanimously, although several people felt that was impossible—but, we did. After the first draft of belief statements were developed, we went to all ethnic and racial groups in their turf to get their reactions. We called the high and middle schools off at noon one day to communicate committees' recommendations to entire student bodies for feedback. We divided kids into groups of about fifteen or twenty high school and middle school kids, and used the same strategy with faculties, aides, and all schools' personnel. Two Planning Committee members met with each group. All suggestions were added to minutes—in red. People could see that their input meant something.

A couple of years later, in a meeting of the Secondary Curriculum Steering Committee (established after this), a high school teacher claimed that he had not been involved. Fortunately, I remembered he was in a group I had met with, and reminded him of it. Heavy involvement paid off. Of 41,000 in the community, including students, about 2,100 were involved.

*Reflective Questions*

1. *What do your neighboring schools state as their purpose?*
2. *Does it drive the school or district?*

With the testing mania in full swing, another current craze is for top-level administrators to state solemnly to boards of education that their prime goal is to raise test scores. Can we raise test scores? Certainly. But as test experts (Lewis 2001) indicate, as soon as a new test is used, scores plummet to original levels.

## What Criteria Can We Develop to Design Common Purposes?

Most purposes come off as slogans, such as "All children will learn." What does that tell you to do? Most mission and purpose statements are so vague as to be meaningless. Here are two more: "The schools will focus on the pursuit of excellence." "All children will reach their highest potential." First, they must be *believable*. Second, they must be *achievable*.

These criteria can move us away from developing pretty sounding, but hollow slogans. Then, the task is to establish vehicles to achieve this.

Finally, after all this feedback, *we adopted the belief statements unanimously*, with their implications for action. (See figure 6.2 for the final document.) Interestingly, at first some were not sure that people would continue to attend meetings, because they had experienced so many organizational failures. As it sunk in that we were succeeding, and that consequences of our deliberations would be far-reaching for teaching and for organizing the schools, committees began to swell.

I also thought that it was essential that the board of education adopt the document—and they did, sending a clear message.

## Belief Statements and Their Implications

These statements have considerable implication for organizing schools and for teaching practices. We said:

1. Each student is different.
    a. Each student learns at a different rate.
    b. Each student has different needs, interests, and abilities and learns from personal interests and curiosity.

These were fundamental, having major implications for reorganizing the actual structure of the schools, teaching, learning, and leadership, including supervision. To achieve these basic beliefs, we stated that we had to:

1. Change our organizational plan to include:
    a. Individualization of instruction.
    b. Learning Resource Centers to facilitate individualizing.
    c. Nongraded approaches [most schools became nongraded]
    d. Independent study models.
    e. . . . technology . . .
    f. Developing flexible scheduling approaches.
    g. Team and cluster organization rather than the self-contained classroom, decentralization is implied.

## Implementation

We spelled out implications for implementation in the third section ("To Implement the Changes . . .") of figure 6.2. These included running in-service

## Goals of the City School District of Long Beach

### These are the guiding beliefs and corresponding educational practices developed by students, faculty, community groups and the Board of Education

Adopted

**BASIC BELIEFS**

1. Each student is different.
   a. Each student learns at a different rate.
   b. Each student has different needs, interests and abilities and learns from personal interest and curiosity.
2. Constant evaluation is necessary if our educational goals are to keep pace with the changing outside world. No subject, method or department is sacred.
3. Learning how to learn, rather than accumulating knowledge, should be a basic tenet of the educational process.
4. People learn responsibility and independence by being given responsibility and independence.
5. The fields of knowledge are related.
6. A primary goal of the educational process is for each student to build a positive self-concept and achieve success.
7. Schools should produce humanistic individuals who are for other people and accept their differences.

**TO ACHIEVE OUR BASIC BELIEFS, WE MUST:**

1. Change our organizational plan to include:
   a. Individualization of instruction.
   b. Learning Resource Centers to facilitate individualizing.
   c. Non-graded approaches.
   d. Independent study models.
   e. Utilizing new technology wisely and effectively.
   f. Developing flexible scheduling approaches.
   g. Team and cluster organization rather that the self-contained classroom, decentralization is implied.
2. Change our approach to curriculum.
   a. Involve many community members in curriculum construction.
   b. Increase number of courses to tie in with individualization of instruction - such as Mini Courses - breaking time to suit our purposes.
   c. Involve leading colleges and universities so that our graduates are not only accepted, but sought after.
   d. Develop a perspective about curriculum to make changes and evaluation on-going and meaningful - a curriculum structure which generates participation and ideas.
   e. Interdisciplinary area studies, major problems, etc., should be the organizing centers for program.
3. Change the role of the teacher.
   a. Differentiated staffing. (Different levels of staff for different purposes.)
   b. Teacher as a learning guide - not a fountain of knowledge.
   c. Utilize the interests and talents of the staff to a greater degree to provide for greater diversity of offerings.

**Figure 6.2.   Belief Statements and Their Implications (*continues*)**

**TO IMPLEMENT THE CHANGES ADVOCATED IN "B", WE MUST IMMEDIATELY:**

1. Provide in-service instruction on the nature of individualized teaching and learning immediately.
2. Operate workshops to assist librarians, CDS's, administrators and teachers to develop learning or instructural resource centers.
3. Run workshops to assist staff in understanding of implementing models of ungraded, independent study, flexible scholarship and team and cluster organization.
4. Implement a curriculum structure before Christmas involving teachers, administrators and supervisors, students and parents.

**TO EVALUATE CHANGES IMPLEMENTED IN "B"**

1. A major administrative focus must be to develop an evaluation scheme which will be inherent in any curriculum.
2. Evaluation should be individualized if program is individualized.

**Figure 6.2.** (*continued*)

seminars to help teachers learn to individualize instruction, use independent study models, move into team teaching, and help everyone learn how to pull off nongrading organizational models. We developed in-services to help librarians move their organizations into instructional resource centers.

We changed your normal, relatively rigid high school All-American six-period schedule into a flexible approach, and reorganized into team teaching instead of typical self-contained classroom structures. We also changed the rigid junior high into a house plan (small learning community or SLC) middle school, saving an administrative position, astonishing the board.

## More Belief Statements, Implications, and Implementation

2. Constant evaluation.
3. Learning how to learn, rather than accumulating knowledge, should be a basic tenet of the educational process.
4. People learn responsibility and independence by being given responsibility and independence.
5. The fields of knowledge are related.
6. A primary goal of the educational process is for each student to build a positive self-concept and achieve success.
7. Schools should produce humanistic individuals who care for other people and accept their differences. [This last belief statement was brought up at the final meeting, recognized as crucial, and adopted by the Planning Committee.]

Note how seriously we took the implications of statement 5, "The fields of knowledge are related." This enabled us to design and implement a complete curriculum-generating structure.

Are these belief statements *believable*? Obviously, children do learn at different rates. Equally patently, children come into school with a considerable variety of interests and a number of different abilities and talents. All we have to do is to reference literature on the seven intelligences (Gardner 1983), now eight. Calvin Taylor (1968), mentioned in chapter 3, has done fascinating work on families of talents people, including kids, display:

- academic (mathematical, analytic, inductive);
- artistic and creative;
- physical (dance, athletic);
- planning and forecasting;
- organizing;
- human relations;
- communicating;
- intuitive; and
- decision making.

Is knowledge unified? Many fields by their titles exemplify this, such as biochemistry, astrophysics, humanities, etc. Interdisciplinary programs and studies abound in some schools, colleges, and universities. We think subjects are separate because in most schools, we teach kids separate subjects (physics, astronomy, math, biology, chemistry).

The next task is to make sure that belief statements are *achievable*. Since children learn at different rates, we can focus on developing programs to help teachers learn how to *individualize* instruction. Immediately, teachers protested they could not teach each kid separately. One comment made by Stanton Leggett (personal communication, April 17, 1971), one of America's premier consultants, was that you individualize through small groups. Once teachers grasped that, we could move. If children (and adults) have different interests, abilities, and talents, then individualized instruction was a strategy that could be used to achieve meeting those.

1. Change our approach to curriculum.
   a. Involve many community members in curriculum construction.

b. Increase number of courses . . . mini-courses . . .
c. Involve leading colleges.
d. . . . a curriculum structure which generates participation and ideas.
e. Interdisciplinary area studies, major problems, etc., should be the organizing centers for the program.


## DESIGNING THE CURRICULUM STEERING COMMITTEE TO GENERATE CHANGE AS A ROUTINE

One major implication for immediate implementation was that a Curriculum Steering Committee had to be designed and adopted so that anyone with an idea could have it considered professionally, rather than being squeezed out because he or she was a teacher, student, or community member with no access to power people. *This structure and process gave everyone a voice.* The purpose was to establish a system that *generated change as a routine*, rather than people having to kill themselves to get an idea implemented.

Somewhat to my surprise, people wanted two Curriculum Steering Committees, an elementary and a secondary model (see figure 6.3), so we proceeded to design models that adopted the same composition of the Planning Committee in order to assure community members and students that they would be able to bring their ideas forth—and *would be heard*.

Note that the composition of five teachers, four students, two administrators, and four community members made power plays impossible to pull off. All three unions chose their representatives, resulting in their supporting the process and the results vigorously. Consequently, we never had rifts over the legitimacy of the process or results. This left administrators and supervisors as a tiny minority—and the processes of sending minutes of every meeting to all social systems were too visible for backroom shenanigans to work.

A couple of months later, I heard that a powerful high school department chairperson was going to deep-six a teacher's proposal, so we met to discuss the norms of our very public agreements.

The document had a one page attachment designed by an English teacher describing the process to bring ideas to Curriculum Steering Committees. It was now in the hands of administrators, teachers, students, and

Progress Report

For the last two months the STEERING COMMITTEE ON GOALS has been involved in intensive study and discussion, pointed to determining our direction and establishing strategic target areas.

> On November 19, the STEERING COMMITTEE adopted a curriculum structure built with broad representation , deliberate flexibility, and avenues of exploration for new ideas and innovations.
>
> Basically, the structure starts with two committees, forming bodies of representation for the elementary and secondary levels.

|  ELEMENTARY | SECONDARY |
|---|---|
| Membership:<br>  5 Teachers: 1 from each school<br>  4 Students:  2 Sr. High<br>           2 Jr. High<br>  1 Administrator<br>  1 Coordinator/Supervisor<br>  1 Pupil Personnel Services rep.<br>  4 Community Adults, including 1<br>     para-professional or aide. | Membership:<br>  5 Teachers<br>  4 Students:  2 Sr. High<br>           2 Jr. High<br>  1 Administrator<br>  1 Coordinator/Supervisor<br>  1 Pupil Personnel Services rep.<br>  4 Community Adults, including 1<br>     para-professional or aide. |

> There will be situations which require the coordination of both committees. In such cases a sub-committee (consisting of representation from both committees) would be drawn together.

The potential profits of such a structure are manifold. This plan provides for awakening and utilizing available resources which have up to now lain fallow. There is "involvement" here -- from within and without the school process – and there is opportunity for interaction and exchange of ideas, followed by systematic study and evaluation. No idea or innovation will be killed or censored before it has a change to be born!

HOW AN IDEA MOVES THROUGH THIS STRUCTURE:

1.  Any one introduces an idea to the elementary or secondary committee, whichever is applicable.
2.  An ad hoc work group (including the originator) is formed by the committee to study the suggestion and develop a proposal.
3.  The proposal is submitted to the curriculum committee for further study, evaluation, recommendation and priority rating to the central administration.
4.  Central administration delivers a final decision after considering the proposal, evaluation, and recommendation.
5.  When the verdict is "GO" and the idea is ready for implementation, appropriate administrators and faculty become involved.
6.  From the moment implementation occurs, it lives with a continuing process of evaluation and re-evaluation.

Figure 6.3.    Curriculum Steering Committee Structure

community to use vehicles established to make changes they thought important. Note assistance available to *anyone* with an idea. Note that it bypassed the leadership structure and went right to one of two Curriculum Committees for action. We thought that was crucial to establish trust that the Curriculum Committees would work, and that no one, from board of education member to administrator, to a supervisor or department chair, could block action.

The Curriculum Steering Committee Structure with four subcommittees (science/math; humanities, including social studies, language arts, fine arts; special areas, such as sex education, special education; and practical arts) was organized and going by early November, to give people a chance to submit ideas that would impact curriculum choices available to faculty and students by the next year. Thus, we had a vehicle organized with massive input and support to change curriculum. The two Curriculum Steering Committee structure differed from other curriculum structures I've designed, which usually consisted of one committee, but it obviously was successful in generating trust and considerable input.

We also kicked in a process of evaluating all proposals and programs.

## IMPLICATIONS FOR TEACHER ROLE

The third implication was to focus on changing the teachers' role. So, we ran workshops, as noted under the implementations section above, to help teachers learn to be facilitators, to individualize instruction through using small groups, to learn team-teaching techniques and attitudes, and independent study skills.

## RESULTS: LESSONS LEARNED

A huge program in the high school exploded from the Curriculum Structure. Teachers, developing greater autonomy, developed quarter courses in virtually all areas, except foreign language, who seemed to resent the process. We generated over eighty courses in the social studies and an equal number in language arts. Many were interdisciplinary, in line with belief statement 5 (the fields of knowledge are related), tying such courses as the Civil War with their English counterparts, with such books as "Andersonville," "Gone with the Wind," and "The Red Badge of Courage." As a matter of fact, all history courses were designed to be interdisciplinary by offering the literature simultaneously, thereby creating a humanities program of no mean significance.

We generated six courses in cultural anthropology, including the best-simulated archaeological dig in the country. A couple of students, after seeing that the process could work, created "Dark Humor," which was passed by the Curriculum Structure, and was taught by the kids supervised by an English teacher. Such courses as "Criminology," "The History of Political Thought and Dissent," and "Liberty in the American Culture" were created and tied in with literary counterparts. "Introduction to Adolescent Psychology" tied in with "Adolescent Love" (featuring Hamlet) in literature.

A dedicated art teacher generated a huge program of about six courses in ceramics, and we pulled in a Japanese seventh generation ceramicist guru to teach for a full year. Science courses generated included such biology teachers' eternal favorites as the fetal pig (beloved by biology teachers and lots of kids), lab techniques, a course on the impact of chemical substances on white mice, etc.

The origins of this last course bear reporting. When I became superintendent a big, angry science teacher with a gravelly voice told me that he had killed himself for three years trying to get a course on white mice on a summer pilot basis, and since he had no political power, he was blocked. He told me that he was giving up, that he wasn't going to waste his time anymore, and would look elsewhere for getting his professional interests met. He said, "In this system, it's who you know, not what you know that gets results."

I indicated that he was right on target, since the system often made decisions on political reasons, often not on what was best for kids and teachers. I told him that it would take about three months to get goals generated, and then we'd set up a curriculum structure where his ideas would get a fair hearing. He said, "Yeah, sure," and walked away angrily, obviously not believing that this young, naïve superintendent could pull that off.

After we had established the curriculum structure, I went to his lab in January, and told him that the time had come for him to take his course proposal to the Secondary Curriculum Committee. He gave me a fish eye, so I asked him for the proposal he had had turned down, said I would submit it to the Science/Math subcommittee, told him that he had the first right of refusal to teach it, and that I would help him with the format necessary to get approval. I added that we could give the course a try this coming summer. He did, it passed, was piloted in the summer quite successfully, and integrated into the course structure that fall. We now, at least, had one genuine convert to constructivism in science.

At first, presentations to the Curriculum Steering Committee tended to be haphazard and informal, but serious questioning established the expertise of the committee, and criteria for accepting a proposal (clear goals and objectives, sample of learning activities, materials needed, time to develop it during the summer, budget, etc.). After a while, presentations became quite polished, and the grapevine told us that people rehearsed their proposals.

After we established the programs, a regional newspaper picked it up and ran the following article (figure 6.4), treating it as a travel package, which we thought was pretty neat. In an example of the Law of Unintended Consequences, the program had an impact on the nonzingy adult education program. My adult friends began to ask why they couldn't have some of the exciting courses we had designed, one actually saying, "What, are we chopped liver?" So, we zinged up the program, and I took one of the ceramics courses run the by the art teacher.

## LESSONS LEARNED—MORE SUCCESSES

### How Was This Constructivist?

Teachers, administrators, students, and community participated in creating courses, on curriculum committees, and selected among the huge array developed. By using flexible scheduling and converting some courses into lab courses (art, computers, vocational courses) students could schedule themselves and sign in by punching a time card to accumulate necessary Carnegie unit credits.

A *system* (Deming 1982) was designed and implemented with maximum involvement of social systems to *generate curriculum change as a*

# How to Fly Package Deal Through High School

If you take four credits in English, four credits in Social Studies, one credit for ninth year science, one credit for Biology, a half credit for Health, one credit in Math, two credits in Physical Education and four and a half credits, with a three year sequence, in electives, you have chosen package number one; and if successfully completed you will have taken eighteen credits of High School studies and will be awarded a Long Beach High School Diploma. However, if you take the same credits as above but instead of four and a half elective credits, you take six and a half elective credits, and you pass the English and Social Studies Regents, you have chosen package deal number two, and will leave the hallways of Long Beach High School with a New York State Regents Diploma. Whatever package deal, you are bound to have a lot of fun, for within each package much like the travel package deals and their choice of hotels, etc., you have an interesting variety of possibilities. A splashing of the '73-'74 Course Offerings at the High School unmask a wonderful journey into the world of knowledge. However, for-warned is forwarded... just like your vacation air flight is only as smooth as the pilot handling the plane and the exotic foods you eat are only as good as the cook who cooks them, so the courses at Long Beach High, intriguingly titled as they are, are only as good as the teaches who teaches them.

Stepping into the English Department, a Sophomore can spend half a year engrossed in Literature and Social Problems reading such

things as Tuned Out and I'm Really Dragged... and can spend the rest of the year in Media and Our World, building fundamentals with films, reading kits and filmstrips. As a Junior and Senior, one may indulge in Quarter courses or Semester Courses. In the Quarterly division there is an opportunity to study Ferlinghetti/Cohen, Arthur Miller, Black Playwrights, Hemingway and a Non-Violence course covering Ghandi/ King/ Baez/ Baker all during one year, with the possibility of having four different teachers, (tour guides) maybe even more if the course is team taught. In the semester division you can choose between diving into fantasy, drama or learning English through the early silent movies or today's fast thrillers. There is even a semester course in English called the 'Good Life.' The course is designed to probe attitudes of self-development, interpersonal relations and changing standards. Students of this course learn Candle making and Flower making as well as work on their communication skills. A bonus to the Good Life course is that you receive credit in English as well as Home Economics.

Bookings in the Social Studies Department can be arranged to visit stones and bones in an anthropological and archeological course, China: from Confucius to Mao, Famous Court Rooms of the World: Dreyfus/ Lt. Calley/ Socrates/ Nuremberg, Hitler's Germany, Russia: Peter the Great to Brezhnev or the World of the Mind: Freud to Bettleheim.

Traveling into the Language Department, land arrangements have

been secured for Latin, German, Spanish, Russian, Italian, Hebrew, Yiddish, and Swahili.

If your trip is being planned with relaxation in mind, the Physical Education Department is the next stop. Swimming, Scuba Diving, Baseball, Football, Tennis, Soccer, Volleyball, Basketball, Lacrosse and Golf can all be arranged.

A student really can't figure out his program by himself. He needs a travel agent. The course at the High School can take his mind so many places, that by college he might have seen the world. Caution should be administered in overloading a student's flight. A couple of days in many countries may confuse the student, and he might not remember more than going into and out of customs. A student should be careful to secure the proper visas in the correct sequence and make certain he leaves Long Beach High School with a passport to the future, not just a postcard to hang on the wall.

LEARN

Figure 6.4.   How to Fly Package Deal through High School
*Source: Nassau Star*

*routine* part of everyday functioning. We made curriculum change a *routine*, thereby finessing problems of resistance.

Change was scheduled into daily activities—and expected to happen. With the structure and process provided, teachers could *design courses they wanted to teach*. So, they jumped in. So did students. People began to work across department lines—the basic structures of schools began to change, becoming *nongraded*. That is, courses were offered to kids on virtually all levels after they satisfied a few basics. We no longer had freshman, sophomore, junior, and senior courses. Maslow's third (social) and fourth (esteem) needs began to be met more adequately by the entire structure and process of curriculum development.

Newspaper articles (figure 6.4) and the reactions of the adult education program were clear signals that we had accomplished something rather significant. By developing an **interest-based curriculum**, it became individualized since people had a huge range of choices.

We certainly paid close attention to **Barnard's three indispensable elements of an organization** (as discussed earlier):

1. Establish a clear mission and purpose.
2. Establish a system of communication to communicate the purpose.
3. Establish a system of cooperation to achieve the mission and purpose.

A supportive culture was created and was itself supported by being written into the contract with the Teachers', Administrators', and Classified Associations so that incoming administrators could not destroy the system.

## SUMMARY

The process worked, the schools got focused, and implications generated by the belief statements were implemented into the system with considerable success. The strange idea that *change ought to occur as a routine* became embedded, so that change processes actually not only became routine, but *were expected to occur routinely*. The elementary schools moved into developing different school models of choice for parent and student decision: One became a multiage ungraded, team-taught model; another became ungraded, but not teamed at first; one became teamed, but graded; and one continued as a self-contained, graded model.

As noted above, the junior high moved into a decentralized SLC hall plan middle school model, began developing interdisciplinary programs, and the high school just exploded its program, so that the idea of being a freshman or junior almost had no meaning. Kids could take virtually any course after minimal requirements were met, because the program became interest-based.

## GLOSSARY

**Barnard's three indispensable organizational elements**   developing a common purpose, and a communication and cooperative system.

**interest-based curriculum**   a curriculum based in interests of students.

**Trump model**   a model for organizing high schools with large-group, small-group, and independent study only; no class-size classes.

## Chapter Seven

# Your First Priority (and Tool)

## How to Establish Yourself with Teachers, Supervisors, Peers, Kids, Community

Only mediocrities rise to the top of a system that won't tolerate wave-making.

—Lawrence Peter

### FROM THE MOUTHS OF BABES

*Reflective Questions*

*1. What do your neighboring schools state as their purpose?*
*2. Does it drive the school or district?*

You must establish yourself. Whether you go into a school as a teacher, as a principal, whether you enter an organization as a student, when you establish a relationship with another person, or with another family, you are faced with establishing yourself.

Do you remember your first day in kindergarten? I do. I remember my mother's face at the door window, looking a bit anxious. I remember waving good-bye, a message that assured her I was OK and she should leave, which she did. When she came at the end of the day to pick me up, she asked how it was, to which I told her it was OK, that we played a lot, that there were some nice kids there, the teacher was nice, and we had cookies and milk, which I liked.

In short, my message was that I felt comfortable in that social system. In light of our present understanding about dynamics of organizations and social systems in writing the above paragraph, my mother interpreted my

waving good-bye to mean that I was comfortable in the process of establishing myself. So, she left.


## THE ORGANIZATION OF THIS CHAPTER

*Reflective Question*

*What tools do we need to work more effectively with basic components of
any organization, the social systems that form their core (this includes
the organization itself)?*

We focus first on *essential issues* all of us face when we enter a group
or social system, including membership identity, power and influence,
goals the group establishes, acceptance, intimacy, and trust. We then have
to decide whether or not we feel that the group's activities have validity
and worth. The next section presents suggestions regarding what to look
for in groups, mentions norms and subcultures, followed by discussing the
value of consensus decision making. Next comes the four-step *P.I.N.C.
decision-making model*, followed by such **group processes** as *participation, morale*, and *influence*, with **group task** *and maintenance functions.*
Next is an anthropologist's "take" on analyzing educational organizations, as if he/she parachuted in from outer space. The last section treats
every educational organization as an *overall system*, with **interrelated
subsystems**. So, by the end of this chapter, you will have quite an armamentarium of tools to analyze, understand, and confidently work with any
group or social system, let alone an educational organization or system.


## ESSENTIAL *ISSUES* ON ENTERING ANY
## ORGANIZATION/SOCIAL SYSTEM (E.G., TRUST)

What, then, are these major issues that we all face on entering any new
group or social system? And, are they universal? That is, whenever we enter any new organization we are inevitably concerned about what will
happen to us, and how new relationships will form. This section is based
on Hensley's (1982) interesting analysis of *issues* we face on entering any

social system. These occur in every group and have considerable potential to impact the life of the group (and ourselves) either positively or negatively (sometimes both). These issues occur sequentially for us upon entering groups. However, they can also emerge randomly or reemerge later.

## Membership Identity

The first issue is that of our identity as a member, since we all wonder immediately when we enter a social system, "Who am I in this group?" And, even more importantly, "Do I want to be here?" Do you remember what you have done in such situations? We sure can feel uncomfortable at first. So, we take a few tentative steps presenting ourselves, psych out roles we might want to play, watch carefully but unobtrusively to see how people are reacting to us—accepting our overtures.

This process can be seen more overtly in kids entering playgroups, where they try to establish themselves. I watched my charismatic daughter, then three years old, meet our new neighbors' five-year-olds. Within two days she was calling out, "C'mon guys, follow me." And they did. She had established herself in a leadership role relatively quickly, which indicates how rapidly social interactions develop, often without our recognizing them.

In such a new situation, we face a somewhat complex developing scenario, since each person often has several different expectations of what is appropriate behavior, and has different role expectations. This is compounded when we interact with a number of people, who obviously have even more differences in their expectations.

Since none of us may be too clear about our expectations, the newbie can feel some anxiety when flung into such a situation (which all of us have faced). As an example, a very funny scene took place in a movie when Richard Pryor and Gene Wilder were thrown into a jail cell with some very large and tough looking "bloods." Half frightened to death, they took the offense by strutting, "We're baaadd, reeeal baaadd." The really tough guys looked pained at the pretense, mostly ignoring the imposters.

Whatever the behavior, the issue of membership identity has to be dealt with, or the social system will continue to be disrupted by people trying to develop their identity as members, and it will remain fixated with that task. Not much else can be accomplished.

## Power and Influence in Formal Groups

Once membership identity has been settled, usually issues of **power and influence** emerge. We wonder who has power in any group, and a corollary of that is, "How much influence can *I* develop?" A somewhat humorous scenario unfolded when I was a superintendent with a committee interviewing candidates for leadership positions. We had a large table in my office, so we decided that an attractive young female teacher should sit behind it, with the rest of us sitting around with the candidate. (I was the second youngest person in the administrative offices, and had a full head of bright red hair then.) We realized shortly that this was unfairly confusing candidates, who could not tell who was superintendent.

As noted in chapter 4, on what makes organizations tick, when we establish any formal group, such as schools, stores, or a gas station, a structure of positions is immediately established. In a school it usually consists of a principal, teachers, a principal's office manager, clerks, students, custodians. Each position has different amounts of formal power allocated, the office manager having more than clerks, head custodians having more than custodians. Usually students lie at the bottom of the pecking order.

To demonstrate how clearly this is grasped even by really young people, my son in second grade expostulated that he did not like having to eat set menus in the cafeteria, while older kids could make choices. He indicated to me that he was perfectly capable of choosing a balanced diet and wanted to be able to make decisions about what he could eat. So, I said, "Well, Marc, why don't you go the principal, and tell him what you would like to do." His response told it all. "I'm just a little kid, you're an adult— besides, you're on the board of education." A seven-year-old understood issues of power and influence.

## Power and Influence in Informal Social Systems

In informal or unstructured groups, who has power and influence has to be worked out—and how it unfolds can have a great deal to do with people's satisfactions—even to the point of whether they will stay. In other words, if people become upset with how power and influence are distributed, and how much or little they get, they may pull out, often leaving really angrily. Owning appropriate quantities of power and influence in our key groups often is pretty important to some of us (well, maybe a lot of us).

So, informal groups face issues of distribution of power and control when new members enter. One way to welcome and to include new people with their myriad of talents may end up with people actually thinking about how to transfer some power to them. Forming subcommittees and allocating various roles to new recruits, especially to those who are considered as important, is one approach. As an example, we can ask, "How can we use Terry's talents?" and then ask her to be involved actively in an important task force. Do you remember when you entered a group wondering how you would establish yourself? What different lines of action could have been undertaken? Did someone help you out? What has been your subsequent relationship with that person who took the role of your sponsor?

## Goals

Once power and control have been settled, people next want to know what the purposes are. And, of course, they ask, are those goals something I can live with? Since each of us may have different purposes, setting clear goals usually is important for groups to continue, let alone to prosper. The downside of that is if people do not buy into the goals, they may withdraw or even sabotage them, something that can raise Cain with accomplishing them.

## Acceptance, Intimacy, and Trust

The next tasks for social systems that become dominant and then must be resolved are acceptance, intimacy, and trust. Almost everyone wants to feel accepted, wants to get closer to some people than others, and has to develop a sense of trust that the group is OK to be in. We enter groups with some fears, often only dimly recognized. We may fear not being accepted, being overpowered (especially the very aggressive members), even of being left out. So, we try to present ourselves as acceptable—and, therefore, liked.

New members do not know the group's dynamics, such as who hangs with whom, the rivalries, so they tend to be disadvantaged, making them vulnerable, and, therefore, uncomfortable. It takes a bit of time to develop a sense of comfort by picking up relationships, and then developing your own niche.

**Trust**

*Reflective Questions*

1. *Of course, do you trust people in the group?*
2. *Whom do you trust first? (Are they pretty much people like you?)*
3. *If you begin to distrust enough people, how long will you stay?*
4. *How fast have you trusted some and not others?*
5. *How do you personally build trust? (By being open or closed with others?)*

## How Essential Is Trust in Any Group?

Do we feel comfortable and open if we do not trust members, key people? Obviously not. Research indicates that establishing trust is essential for groups to prosper (see chapter 11). How, then, do we establish trust? Exercises I use point to being open with others, which, in turn, generally causes others to become more open. The dynamic of being open is that we trust the others, leading them to become more open — and trusting.

## Do the Group's Activities Have Validity and Worth?

The last issue faced by new members (and, often, old), is whether the group's activities are worthwhile. People must feel that what they are doing is important. My wife and I were invited to join an informal group by a friend to promote buying American goods. However, she thought (later joined by me), that this was doomed to failure, and declined to be involved, much to the friend's discomfort. The next time you join a group note whether you feel that their activities are worthwhile. If not, did you try to change the activities — or did you leave?

## DIFFERENT WAYS TO VIEW SOCIAL SYSTEMS: ANOTHER TOOL

Remember, we are dealing with *tools* people use to become more effective leaders.

**What Are Some Keys to Look for in Groups?**

Some of the following is based on insights from "What to Look for in Groups" (Hanson 1972). In the next two sections, you might want to take the role of the astute observer who is watching *processes* in groups unfold. Most of us have been conditioned to look for the *content* that develops as social systems interact. Of at least equal importance are the processes that occur, since they determine how the social systems operate. Another term often used refers to the *dynamics* that develop as people in groups interact, that is, group dynamics. These consist of such things as:

- norms, subcultures (discussed in chapter 4), and feelings;
- participation;
- morale;
- influence (see the next chapter);
- decision-making approaches;
- leadership styles and struggles;
- conflict, competition, and cooperation;
- task and maintenance functions; and
- subgrouping.

In chapter 4, "What Makes Organizations Tick?," we discussed different norms and subcultures that groups form, which, of course, are key to looking at its health. To this, we can add feelings, so that we as observers have to be aware of feelings that arise as people interact, and how people treat each other.

**Norms, Subcultures, Feelings**

Remember, norms consist of customs people develop, while subcultures consist of clusters of norms. In high schools usually students take a variety of classes run by different teachers, while kindergarteners work and play in one room with one teacher and, perhaps, an aide. Big difference. And, different subcultures develop in both. The following are just a few questions and issues it is useful to become aware of.

*Reflective Questions*

1. *Do people accept, like, reject, support, attack each other?*
2. *What is dealt with, avoided, such as sex, politics, religion, the leader's behavior, negative behavior, in conversations?*
3. *What norms have developed in your schools? Do you like them?*
4. *Can you change some? What is tolerated, what is not?*
5. *Is the subculture the same in the central office, elementary schools, high school(s)?*
6. *How different is the culture in a Wal-Mart, FBI, a gas station, from a typical elementary school?*

The key is that we can help create norms in our social systems—if we become conscious about it, and know how to do it.

## Participation

Who participates, who does not? How is each person treated? Is it OK to be silent? If so, does this extend over all areas? Is being silent taken as consent, disagreement, fear? Who keeps the ball rolling? Do some focus more on tasks, while others more on feelings? This is a normal role split in groups. Who takes the role of life of the party? The clown? The distracter? Is there a dominator?

## Morale

Morale is often perceived as group persistence, compared with **esprit de corps**, which is group feeling (Blumer 1963). Esprit de corps has shorter cycle ups-and-downs, while morale is the stuff that makes for long-term persistence in achieving goals. The U.S. Marines usually have both.

*Reflective Questions*

1. *What is the condition of morale and esprit de corps in your group? Major organizations? Who are key architects of each?*

2. *How does the **group maintain** morale? What groups have you been in that have high morale? What has been your role?*
3. *How do administrators create and destroy morale?*
4. *What does your leader do? How about you?*

## Influence

Influence is interesting. Who has considerable influence in your groups? Some people may not participate, but exert influence. Do you? How can you increase yours? You can often tell who has influence by how people listen, or not, as people in the group interact.

How about rivalry? This gets at factions in social systems, and picks up struggles for leadership. Is one going on in your groups? What is your role? Do you want a role in struggles that may occur in groups in which you live?

## Value of Consensus Decision Making

How are decisions made? I once was superintendent where often only one person on the board of education expressed an idea about a decision, which sometimes carried the day. Does the group have decent respect for minority viewpoints?

Has the group decided that a majority will carry the day, or that major decisions need consensus? If you go this way, consensus-seeking takes more time since people have to become comfortable with the one decision, but in the end, this approach makes sense since a minority is not created. This process creates no losers.

H. A. Thelen (personal communication, 1958) pointed out the value with the following diagram (figure 7.1):

Which is longer? Note that if a decision is made by yourself (or one person), you may never convince the rest. You may constantly be dealing with feelings from the fallout of that unilateral decision, which is why it may take so long (or never) to convince others. That diagram convinced me of the value of taking the time to make decisions by consensus, if at all possible. The problem with calling for a vote is that it tends to generate minorities.

_____

Time It Takes to Make a Decision by Yourself

_____

Time It Takes to Make a Consensus Decision

_____  _____

Time It Takes to Convince Others That Your Decision Should Be Followed

**Figure 7.1.   The Time It Takes to Make a Consensus Decision: Its Value**

*Reflective Questions*

1. *Has this been a norm? What happens if people lose several votes?*
2. *Does the group stay on one topic, or does it jump around? What is the impact on decision making? On frustration levels? Why does the group do this?*
3. *Who supports whom? How does the group view them? Do they often do this?*

Decision making may be more complex than is apparent. Shapiro, Benjamin, and Hunt (1995) developed a quick, but effective four-step or phase decision-making strategy in organizations with the acronym P.I.N.C. (see figure 7.2). This perspective views decision making in organizations as a social enterprise, not being made by an individual alone on a mountain top, but working in concert.

1. *When confronted with an issue, people think about it—the* Problem *phase.*
2. *When they see it is important, they* Interact, *since the* Problem *has to be solved. (You cannot decide all alone on a major solution and implement it by yourself in organizations without consequences.)*
3. *As solutions emerge from Interactions, people begin to* Negotiate *which should prevail.*
4. *As these end in a decision, we look at* Consequences.

As a result, the cycle may begin again. Clearly, this is a *social decision-making process*, but what decisions made in social systems are not social?

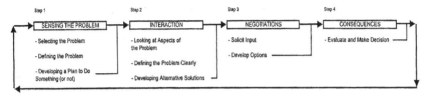

**Figure 7.2.    Steps in the Decision-making Process (Generic) P.I.N.C.**

## More Group Processes: Conflict, Competition, and Cooperation

Anthropologists noted that when cultures collide, they first generate a good deal of conflict (colonists with Indians), then they begin to compete, often with a good deal of hostility, which anthropologists called accommodation, hostile cooperation. Next, they learn the benefits of cooperation in order to achieve their ends.

Which occurs most frequently in your groups? In marriages of your relatives and friends? In yours? Which is most productive in achieving your and your groups' goals?

Obviously, trust is a major underpinning of how we work well together—and it takes a long time for trust to be established, but is it worth it! Without trust, we simply watch very carefully what other people are up to. If we are not sure about people and their intentions, or we do not trust them, we often sit across from them to watch them. Where do you sit at meetings with people you do not trust or like? Those you do trust?

Americans, with our individualistic philosophy, put great emphasis on competition. In my classes, often even after we do exercises on confrontation and trust-building, some believe that competition is inherent. Actually, some cultures (some American Indian societies), will not tolerate competition. Teachers from the American mainstream often ruin themselves with these kids when they try to reward those who finish first. If you look at any team, if they cannot cooperate, they will not have success (the Boston Red Sox in Ted Williams's era), but this is often lost on our individualistically focused colleagues. Teams must learn to cooperate to be top-notch, whether they are athletic teams, sales teams, restaurant kitchens, or teaching teams.

## Accomplishing Tasks and Maintaining the Group

Groups have to achieve tasks, so that focus is crucial. But, equally vital is dealing with people's feelings. We need people who check on our feelings in groups, such as asking if everyone is OK with a decision. Organizations missing people who focus on their emotional health do not do well, often ending with people feeling angry, often embittered.

The emotional health of a group is crucial to its success and continuation. It certainly is necessary for a high degree of morale to construct positive working relationships so that people can contribute successfully to the processes, and thereby create an effective team who trusts each member.

Benne and Sheats (1948) developed a series of role functions for both the task and the maintenance of groups. Positive task functions include:

- information seeker;
- opinion giver;
- summarizer of the discussion; and
- energizer.

Maintenance functions include:

- gatekeeper;
- expeditor (so that more people participate);
- encourager of participation;
- group observer;
- commentator (the modern version of the Greek chorus); and
- harmonizer.

Last, they cited idiosyncratic functions, which do not meet individuals' needs, but obstruct completing the task or maintaining the group:

- aggressor;
- blocker;
- recognition seeker; and
- playboy.

## Subgrouping (Really, Social Systems)

It seems relatively clear that groups will inevitably divide into subgroups, that people will hang together with those with whom they are comfortable. The astute person will pick up on this to work more effectively. Missing these relationships can produce difficulties. Whom do you like to hang around with? Are they people you trust?

## OUTSIDE THE BOX: AN ANTHROPOLOGIST ANALYZES SOCIAL SYSTEMS

So far, we've talked about analyzing social systems essentially from the perspective of being a participant. What if we could look "outside the box" in our quest to become more objective? That is precisely the function of the anthropologist, who almost appears as if he/she had parachuted in from another planet with insights. That specialist looks at social systems as an outsider, asking fundamental questions.

*Reflective Questions*

1. *What are purpose(s) of social systems called schools?*
2. *How are they expressed in leaders' and teachers' behavior—is there a disconnect?*
3. *For what roles and responsibilities in the culture are schools educating students?*
4. *What is its relationship to the community? Peripheral? Central?*
5. *What message do architectural features convey? Does the building have tall fences?*
6. *What messages do hallways, classrooms convey? Are they light, inviting, dark?*
7. *Who is in control in the boxes (read, classrooms)? Who asks questions?*
8. *Who decides what issues people in the boxes deal with?*
9. *Who does most of the talking and answering?*
10. *Are kids active, or mostly sit, listen?*

In short, we are trying to figure out roles and responsibilities of students and teachers. For example, what inferences can be made about behaviors the culture values from your observations? What kinds of models of adult behavior does the school display; how do they relate to professed political beliefs? In short, do schools and teachers demonstrate democratic values? Who sets disciplinary rules? Principals? Teachers? Do students have a say? Which adults and students appear to be honored? Are all or only some students honored? How does this relate to political beliefs? What rites and rituals does the school enact, such as homecoming, spirit bonfires, and honors assemblies? Obviously, we could ask many more questions. Which would you ask to get the hang of the school's values?

## MORE TOOLS: USING SYSTEMS THEORY AS YOUR PRISM TO UNDERSTAND SCHOOLS

Luciano's (1979) brief article is the basis for this discussion, citing five subsystems to peer into the dynamics of organizations (see figure 7.3). He noted, "The systems view is a way of thinking about the job of management by considering the organization as an *integrated whole* made up of *interacting parts*." Thus, all subsystems are interrelated and force the observer to view the entire organization as a whole, rather than the piecemeal approaches many unconsciously often take. This enables us to see that changing any system may affect another system, or all systems. Often changes may be made that appear innocent or limited, but have considerable impact on other systems.

### The Environmental Subsystem

The environmental subsystem involves all factors external to the organization, from legal systems to political/governmental systems such as city building codes, sources of finances, religious systems, etc. If we are talking about a single school, the district and school form part of the environment.

### The Psychosocial Subsystem

Much of this book comprises this subsystem, since it consists of individuals and groups within the school, and includes peoples' values, attitudes, beliefs, personal and social behavior, motivation, group dynamics, con-

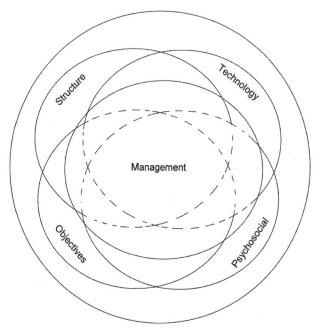

**Figure 7.3.   The Systems View of Organizations: Dynamics of Organizational Change**
*Source:* P. R. Luciano, 1979. *Annual Handbook for Group Facilitators,* ed. John E. Jones & William J. Pfeiffer. Reprinted by permission of John Wiley & Sons., Inc.

flicts, relationships with others. It obviously consists of the subculture of the school and community, and so includes trust, and the like.

## The Structural Subsystem

While smaller groups may not have much of a structure, organizations as complex as schools generate structures, such as lines of authority, communication structures and processes, and tables of organization. Similarly, organizations create informal structures equally important to deal with and understand. This informal organization also generates lines of communication and informal authority. One district called its central administration restaurant, "The Grape Vine."

## The Objectives Subsystem

These comprise goals and purposes for which the school or organization was developed. In the last few years we have seen all sorts of mission statements emerge, many of which obviously resemble the quest for motherhood, apple pie, and the Holy Grail in their practicality. I like to read mission statements of schools, districts, and organizations, usually on their entrance walls. Usually, no one else reads or pays attention to them. If I ask people about it, they usually are clueless, the statements often are so general that they are meaningless as a driving force.

## Technological Subsystem

These days, huge chunks of funding get allocated to technology in most districts. Some research has indicated that technology often does not have as much impact on learning as we would like, although we continue to hope that the next great technological advance will make Herculean progress for the kiddies.

## The Managerial Subsystem

For us in the leadership arena, this constitutes a key area, since this subsystem is involved in organizing and often in controlling other subsystems. This probably is the reason why we study such phenomena as power, authority (see the next chapter), communication systems, decision-making systems (note these in previous sections), plus other leadership functions and phenomena such as supervising and planning.

## STRATEGIES (COURTESY OF THE HILLSBOROUGH MASTERS COHORT)

## Group 1

- Be accessible.
- Be open to new ideas.
- Get noticed—by volunteering for high visibility committees—and work hard.
- Listen.
- Know/be yourself.

## Group 2

- Observe dynamics.
- Informal leaders.
- Group roles.
- Culture.
- Be vulnerable.
- Build trust.
- Share yourself.
- Follow through.
- Do what you say.
- Be humble.
- Don't be a know-it-all.

## Group 3

- Set expectations—let them be known.
- Introduce yourself—participate in social activities (be visible).
- Attend professional learning/development communities (PLCs)—be part of team meetings; allow input.
- Organization/communication; let people know how to contact you, your schedule.

## Group 4

- Feed them.
- Listen to them.
- Visit them.
- Support their decisions.
- Get to "know" them and their families.
- Do what you say.
- Follow up and follow through.
- SMILE.

## Group 5

- Get involved.
- Join professional organizations.

- Network.
- Get community involvement.
- Identify group roles.
- Team player/leader.
- Patience.

## Group 6

- Be known for kind/courteous acts (preparing coffee, picking up trash, giving compliments, always smiling).
- Be knowledgeable about our profession.
- Be a part of organizations (PDK, PTO, etc.).
- Provide novel solutions/perspectives to problems that arise.
- Always be on time, be understanding about the "human condition."
- Always wear colorful clothing (as a signature of your style).

## Group 7

- Smile.
- Open door.
- Be flexible.
- Be positive.

### SUMMARY

It's about time we summarize. We presented a number of key tools to assist us to become better practitioner-leaders, with a particular focus on establishing ourselves. First, we laid out some major issues we face when entering any social system, such as developing membership identity, psyching out and maybe developing power and influence, identifying its goals, its acceptance, intimacy and trust, and deciding whether the activities have validity and worth.

We presented some key phenomena (fancy terminology for things) to look for, such as norms, the organization's subcultures, feelings in it, patterns of participation and morale and influence, the value of consensus approaches, the four-stage P.I.N.C. decision-making model, the nature of conflict, competition, and cooperation, and the necessity of focusing on achieving tasks while maintaining the emotional health of social systems.

We then briefly peered through the anthropologist's eyes to grasp the essential nature of organizations, particularly those whose main mission is education. Almost finally, we treated systems theory with its five subsystems as another tool to improve our professional practice. And finally, grad students in a cohort working in groups developed a series of strategies to establish ourselves.

## GLOSSARY

**esprit de corps**   high levels of group spirit, shorter than morale.

**group maintenance**   concern for the feelings of participants.

**group task**   concern for achieving the tasks and goals of the group.

**group processes**   interpersonal processes in groups, such as participation, decision making, conflict, acceptance.

**interrelated subsystems**   the subsystems in any organization, such as teams in a league.

**morale**   group persistence over time to achieve its goals.

**power and influence**   see chapter 8.

## Chapter Eight

# Power, Empowering, and Constructivist Leadership

How Do You Get It? How Can You Use It? Grow It?
Lose It? (Which Is Pretty Easy to Do)

Power tends to corrupt, and absolute power corrupts absolutely.

—Lord Acton

How long did it take for them to realize who's in charge here? One day.

—Jimmie Jones, former head coach of the Miami Dolphins

## POWER AND AUTHORITY: CONDITIONS FOR IT TO EXIST

All of us have watched people in leadership positions come into a new job—and in as little as two months blow it, losing the support of their staff and colleagues. Others prosper. What's the difference?

This is somewhat easy (if you understand the sources and bases of **power**, **authority**, and **influence** and their relationship to constructivist practices), so let's figure out what they are all about—how we get them—and can lose them. Then, we can take a look at the constructivist use of power.

Most people still believe when they take a leadership position that *their power comes from their supervisor.* That's why most people in leadership positions look steadily toward their superiors, rather than toward their subordinates. Is that a mistake? Let's look at another way of viewing this, a way of thinking that appears quite radical, even to us moderns.

Keeping with our theme (borrowed from Lambert et al. 1995, 1996) that constructivist leadership is based on *relationships (the key)*, so are power, authority, and influence, as seen from various formulations we cite. Thus, we are switching from the common view of *power and control over others to our relationships with others*, almost (well, actually) a *paradigm* shift.

If you've read chapters 4 and 6, you've figured out that Barnard (1938) is a basic source for a great deal of thoughtful, good leadership practice. His unusual analysis of power and authority, particularly when he wrote, supports this.

Barnard thought that the basis for leaders developing authority and power rested on their *communications being accepted* by subordinates. The subordinate has to *perceive* the communication as authoritative and has to *accept it*. We have suddenly moved into communications theory and group dynamics to understand power and authority. That's quite a shift in thinking that power is endowed by our superiors. Barnard is saying the opposite, *authority must be accepted by subordinates* for it to exist.

Four conditions must exist for communications to be authoritative:

1. The communication has to be understood by subordinates.
2. The communication cannot be inconsistent with subordinates' perceptions of the organization's purposes.
3. Subordinates have to perceive the communication as consistent with their purposes.
4. Subordinates have to be able to carry out the communication both mentally and physically.

Let's look at the far-reaching implications of this. If we are to develop power and authority, people must *believe* we have it—so, we must be aware that all four conditions are operating. The key is that subordinates must *accept* communications without full, rational analysis of options. Subordinates accept decisions because they come from a source vested with the *right* to make decisions or communications.

*If they accept it*, we have authority and power. If not, we have neither. If the latter, that becomes extremely serious since we have lost our authority; people may not accept orders or directions from us. We're really in deep trouble, especially if nonacceptance spreads. Examples abound, some of high drama.

*Reflective Questions*

1. *How about the Abu Ghraib prison torture in Iraq?*
2. *Would this have occurred if American troops believed that torturing people was inconsistent with the U.S. Army's purposes?*
3. *Or, with their own beliefs and purposes (Barnard's third condition)?*

In the Iraq War, American troops have been extremely careful to avoid shooting into mosques unless fired on, an example of the second principle. It is not the purpose of U.S. military to defile religious buildings.

When Mark Antony abandoned his ships and troops at the Battle of Actium, he obviously felt that following Cleopatra (who left the battlefield) was consistent with his purposes. His troops abandoned him because they felt the same way. If it was consistent with his purposes to abandon them, it was equally within their purposes to do the same.

## POWER, AUTHORITY, AND INFLUENCE COMPARED

How many of us use power, or authority, rather than influence? I was first turned on to the value of influence as an adolescent when I read Robert Maynard Hutchins, the chancellor of the University of Chicago, probably the most influential university president in the United States in the twentieth century, writing that he largely tried to influence people. I really didn't quite understand this until I moved into leadership positions and worked on a doctorate. It crystallized more clearly when reading Max Weber's (1946) work on power, authority, and influence (see figure 8.1).

Weber, a late nineteenth- and early twentieth-century sociologist, focused on *influence* over others' behavior, which he saw as having two parts: *involuntary* and *voluntary compliances.* Involuntary compliance he perceived based on power, *forced compliance.* Power rests on threats, or actual use of physical force, or manipulation of social or economic conditions.

Authority and influence are based on *voluntary compliance.* Authority is willingly obeyed because people, recognizing authority as legitimate,

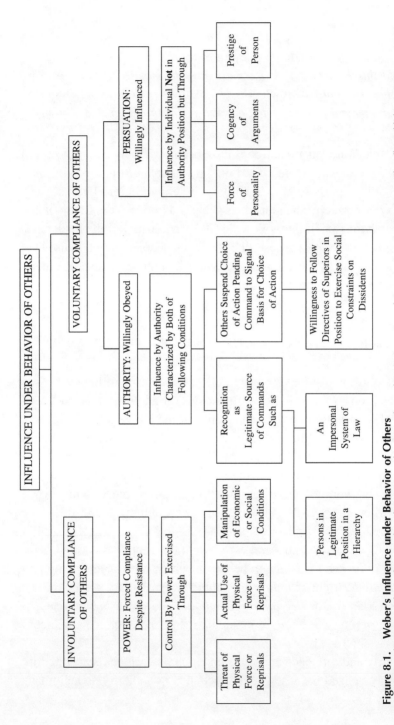

**Figure 8.1. Weber's Influence under Behavior of Others**

*Source:* Based on Max Weber's Theoretical Analysis presented in P. M. Blau and W. R. Scott, *Formal Organizations* (San Francisco: Chandler Publishing, 1962), pp. 27–32. Reprinted by permission of Pearson Education.

suspend their critical and rational thinking to choose alternatives. Persuasion is based on influence through one's force of personality, cogency of arguments, or prestige. For Weber, it pays to be charismatic and/or a **reference** (prestigious and respected) **person**.

## SOURCES OF POWER: FRENCH AND RAVEN

Before we jump to any fast conclusions, let's look at French and Raven's (1959) formulation of sources of power. They perceived a number of sources (I've added a couple, and borrowed several from Lambert, et al. (1996) citing Dunlap and Goldman (1991) and the last three listed, Bolman and Deal (1991):

* Legitimate or position power—one gets by becoming a principal.
* Reward power—limited, because it wears off. Kids want more M&M's; teachers want more pay.
* Expertise or knowledge—if you're a budgetary expert, you know where the bodies are buried, so people respect you.
* Tradition—a basis for position power. We respect people's positions, offices.
* Referential power—takes a long time to build high degrees of respect that you're a person of considerable substance. Who are your reference persons?
* Charismatic power—President Kennedy's charisma lasts. Great power base.
* Love—which of your teachers has great power and influence over you? Your parents?
* Modeling—after whom do you model yourself? Which teacher, leader? Often, we're unaware of this. I used to like wearing tweed jackets, modeled after my major professor, Roald F. Campbell, of the University of Chicago.
* Facilitative (Dunlap and Goldman 1991).
* Alliance and networks—helps to have allies and friends.
* "Access to and control of agendas—access to decision-making arenas."
* Control of meaning and symbols—defining what the group values.

Since a key to constructivism rests on people making meaning together, collaboratively, the last point, defining what the group values and develops common symbols and meanings, is a key point. Collaboration in developing common meanings is the key to constructivist use of power. To that, Lambert, et al.'s (1996) perception of supporting relationships as the foundation of leadership adds power in a shared vision and in personal commitment, nurturing relationships and growth in others, and partnerships that grow.

## A DEFINITIVE (AND SIMPLE) STATEMENT OF SOCIAL POWER—ROBERT BIERSTEDT

Bierstedt (1950), a good sociologist, focused on *social* power, with a relatively simple approach. Bierstedt (as we do) perceived organizations as *social* entities, *as socially constructed realities*. As pointed out in chapters 4, 5, and 6, once any organization is formed, positions and roles are immediately created and once created, some have more and others less power, authority, and influence, at least in Western society.

Bierstedt's simple-appearing contribution follows:

* Power is *institutionalized authority*;
* Authority, in turn, rests on the *capacity* to apply sanctions; and
* Sanctions are *stored force*.

Short, pithy, isn't it?

### Applications of Bierstedt

Let's see how this works, so we can function more effectively. Social power for Bierstedt ultimately rests on one's *capacity* to apply force. The underbelly of this is once we use power—if it fails—we're up the creek. We have lost our power—immediately. By perceiving power this way, it is a predisposition or a prior *capacity to employ* force. Power, therefore, is *potential*. It is essentially *stored force*, the ability to use force.

Why are militaries so cautious about using force? Because if it fails, they (and we) do not have it anymore. So, the actual reason for the existence of military, the application of force to establish authority and power, is something they resist. They fear that if using force fails, they lose their power—inevitably. A quick illustration? The destruction of Iraq's army.

## Reflective Question

*How can we continue to apply these formulations regarding authority, power, and influence to leadership behavior, especially constructivist behavior?*

Statements of an intention to use force or power must be perceived as absolutely certain to be used. If not, they ring hollow. Thus, students, off-spring, teachers, must perceive that sanctions absolutely will be applied. From these formulations, everyone can learn a great deal. Unless threats are perceived as genuine, that they absolutely will be carried out, one's power is certain to be diminished.

As a parent, I never took a position with my kids that I perceived they would ignore, because I knew that once my power and authority were questioned, they would evaporate. Besides, by then, I realized that influence and authority and developed shared meanings in the family were the best avenues to pursue, as Hutchins recommended.

Internalizing Bierstedt's formulations of power, authority, and force is useful in my professional practice. I always stated very matter-of-factly when issues of power and authority rose, "Look, I want you to know I'm not threatening you. If you will do this, then I will do the following. It's your choice."

It's a surefire way to establish credibility—and to head off foolish challenges, power plays, and attempts to dominate. Of course positional and charismatic power and authority backed my hand in impending showdowns. This approach had to be taken with extreme rarity, and only with people who did not know me too well.

## More Applications: Why the "War on Drugs" Is a Bust

So, why is the so-called war on drugs a complete bust? Authorities have been unable to convince all of us that we certainly will be caught, since for the most part—we're not. The threat of immediate use of sanctions (stored force) is simply not believed, so large numbers of people in all socioeconomic classes and ages use drugs. If we use Weber's formulation, people simply do not believe that physical force will be applied to them.

Lambert cites Macy (1994–1995), listing six widespread myths about power. Hopefully, this analysis has destroyed all of them.

1. Power is a scarce commodity . . . only some have it.
2. Power and authority are vested solely in positioned leaders.
3. For me to have power, I have to reduce yours.
4. Power is forcing one's will on another and reducing choices for others.
5. Building defenses makes us powerful.
6. Having power gives one the ability to legislate meaning and fix identity.

## Constructivist Leadership and Power (Briefly)

So, what's the handle that constructivism gives us regarding power, influence, and authority? If we grasp the notion that forming relationships is the basis for constructivist leadership, we're on the money. Involvement, building partnerships with our colleagues, and, therefore, building trust becomes the foundation for empowerment. We now have the keys for power, influence, and authority: building relationships becomes the source for constructivist leadership—the rest follows.

## SUMMARY

This is simple. It turns out to be extremely useful to understand sources of power, and the various formulations about the nature of authority, power, and influence and their relationship to constructivist leadership to practice our craft more effectively. Fortunately, we have some pretty decent useful guidelines for our professional practice.

## GLOSSARY

**authority** based on communications (from Barnard 1938).

**influence** either voluntary or involuntary compliance, according to Weber (1946).

**power** capacity to employ force (from Bierstedt 1950).

**reference person** a person with great prestige and respect to whom we listen.

*Section IV*

# A THREE- (NOW FIVE-) YEAR CASE STUDY OF CONSTRUCTIVIST LEADERSHIP

We don't see things as they are; we see things as we are.

—Anaïs Nin

## Chapter Nine

# A Three-Year Constructivist Case Study

## Part 1

To accomplish great things, we must not only act but also dream, not only plan but also believe.

— Anatole France

Help me—I'm drowning!!

—Lynne Menard, assistant principal and Berbecker Fellow

### COMPARING TEACHERS' STATEMENTS IN CHAPTERS 9 AND 10

Chapter 10 presents the school three years (now five years) later, after it became constructivist. A subsequent study two years later determined if the school retained its constructivist philosophy and teaching practices.

*Reflective Question*

*What do you do when a high-energy elementary principal, starting her doctorate, asks you to help resolve conflict between a group of excellent teachers, who had come from a widely known and celebrated school with an equally competent veteran faculty? She also wanted to move the entire large school toward constructivist instruction.*

Both these comments got my attention. Better have a good change strategy in your hand (or, your head). Fortunately, I did.

151

# ORGANIZING FOR CHANGE

## Outside Facilitator

The principal noted that to focus on needed priorities, it was necessary to involve someone in organizational development to facilitate discussion and analysis, particularly when issues and problems are complex. Bringing in outside facilitators is supported by literature (Beckhard 1969; Mintzberg 1994).

Sitting down with the principal was a first step, particularly focusing on *concerns and issues* people felt. First, of course, we chatted about each other.

## The Principal

She was one of a declining number of female principals in a Western state, migrated for a change of scenery, served several years as a teacher to become certified in a new state, did it with a sense of humor, underwent a year as an intern principal, and finally, became a principal. When the district decided to build a new school, she was chosen as principal.

One reason was the district's confidence in her. Teachers joked that the district left her alone, because she was obviously so competent. Being unassuming, she thought that was amusing. People knew that she was not afraid to take risks (for example, moving in midcareer to a new state where she first had to become a teacher to qualify as a principal, an administrative intern next).

## A Major (and Unexpected) Source of Conflict

One source of conflict was that a group of new people, all excellent teachers, suffered huge disappointments in their former school as its widely heralded mission for which they were recruited nationally, and to which they were deeply committed, changed rapidly into a traditional school.

Consequently, feeling betrayed, they came into this school feeling defensive, "coming in with their guns blazing." As a result, perfectly normal organizational processes immediately surfaced, such as issues of trust/distrust, we/they (acceptance/rejection), and defensiveness.

When groups enter organizations, conflict often occurs based upon perceived differences between old and new groups for a variety of predictable reasons. Experienced people often are hired to enrich the organization; however, with experience comes their own set of norms, which can be perceived as threatening to the established subculture. Because these folks entered as a group rather than individuals who could be more easily assimilated, their impact was greater.

## Resolving This

The change strategy, reflection, and dialogue helped people realize that apparent conflicts in norms and beliefs did not exist. The new folks referred to methods of instruction by different labels, which led to a buildup of resentment since the newbies were perceived as trying to take over. Once teams discussed specific reading strategies, rather than specific labels, resistance regarding instructional differences vanished. It was still necessary to build trust before discussions as near to the heart of teachers as instructional strategies could become productive.

## The School—Briefly

The large elementary school, with over nine hundred students, was in its third year, with a growing community mostly of people living in homes, with increasing immigrants from a variety of cultures and nations. Socioeconomically, it was middle and working class.

## USING THE ANALYSIS OF DYNAMICS OF ORGANIZATIONAL CHANGE: A DIAGNOSING, ANALYZING, PLANNING, AND IMPLEMENTING STRATEGY

This **Analysis of Dynamics of Organizational Change** model and planning process flowed out of work with several schools and a hospital. Actually, as I was working with faculty and administration in each school, trying to grasp the complexities of two schools, the model fell out. I stepped back from the chart paper sheets on the wall, and thought, "Holy smoke, I've come up with a bottom-up change model!" Obviously, it is a constructivist change strategy since it works from teachers' input. It is also **Lewinian** (1952a) since it breaks the system out of present practices, moves to a new level, and refreezes the new norms/culture.

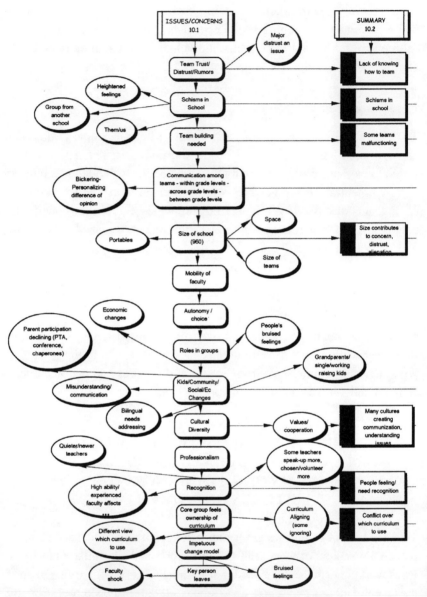

**Figure 9.1.** Analysis of Dynamics of Organizational Change (*continues*)

## An Individualized Constructivist Change Model

It's considerably beyond a simple change strategy, enabling one first to *diagnose and analyze* any organization's Issues and Concerns, next to Summarize them, and then to dig away at Underlying Themes. The fourth step

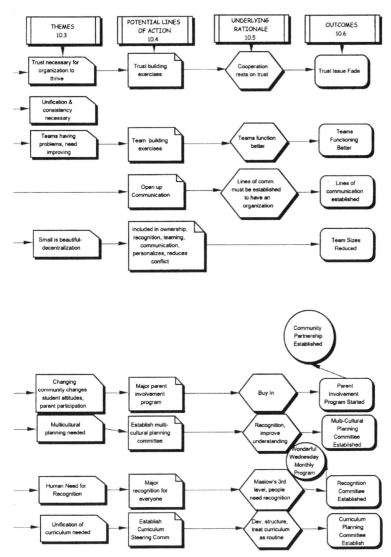

**Figure 9.1.** (*continued*)

is to develop **Potential Lines of Action**, (a Plan) to deal with them, next to look at Underlying **Rationales** for each Line of Action, and last to analyze Consequences and Outcomes of implementing the plan as it evolves (see figure 9.1).

In short, it is a highly *individualized* constructivist bottom-up change strategy in stark contrast with most attempts, which try to change organizations top-down, the usual strategy for most national foundations' efforts, our own national efforts, such as Goals 2000 and No Child Left Behind (NCLB), and many state change strategies, such as Florida's Comprehensive Assessment Test (FCAT) (see Hunt, Benjamin, and Shapiro 2004, for teachers' perceptions about a change strategy shoved down their throats).

All, of course, are fatally flawed, since they use one change strategy to try to force very complex organizations to move in a direction they've decided upon. And the inhabitants resist, at which they are very good!

States, which use tests to force districts to move in directions they unilaterally and politically decide upon, generally find the teaching profession vigorously opposed to such coercion. Individual schools and districts who use top-down change strategies generally have them implemented by only a few true believers, who usually leave after a short while because they get sick and tired of the slings and arrows aimed their way. The Annie E. Casey Foundation's attempt reveals this (Wehlage, Smith, and Lipman 1992), as does the Coalition of Essential Schools (Muncey and McQuillan 1993).

This diagnostic, analytic, implementation, and change strategy is a process of Organizational Mapping, uncovering processes organizations generate in their functioning. The resultant figure I titled "The Analysis of Dynamics of Organizational Change" (Burley and Shapiro 1994; Shapiro, Benjamin, and Hunt 1995; Shapiro 2000b).

In addition, modeling constructivist thinking requires focusing on higher cognitive levels, such as dealing with Concerns and Issues, analyzing Underlying Themes, constructing a Plan to deal with Issues and Concerns, analyzing Outcomes, and finally evaluating them.

*Reflective Question*

*How similar is this process of getting accepted as discussed in chapter 7, on how to establish yourself?*

- The first stage, informal, of course, is to get people's confidence, particularly those able to make decisions. Otherwise, you're out on your ear.
- The next step, still informal, is to get a representative Planning Committee of key people who are trusted and represent all shades of opinions and feelings. (If you stack the deck by making it unrepresentative, you will destroy its and your credibility.)

- Next, we have to get at Underlying Concerns and Issues people perceive. This takes time, and cannot be rushed, otherwise we will miss something crucial. These Concerns and Issues have to be written on large sheets of chart paper for the Planning Committee to see. Then, they must be reduced to $8\frac{1}{2}'' \times 11''$ paper, and sent to *everyone* (and, I mean, everyone—or, the uninformed will get upset, suspicious, and harm the effort), teachers, PTA, office staff, ensuring immediate effective *communication* (shades of Barnard) to one and all. No one can be left out—or, they will feel, and be, left out. When it comes time to need their support—they won't be there!
- The succeeding step is to Summarize those many Concerns and Issues.
- Next, we analyze Underlying Themes, which unify the inquiry, and which also winnow down insights into a few manageable factors.
- Next, we try to figure out Potential Lines of Action/Initiatives to take action to resolve Issues/Concerns and Themes.
- We then work at figuring out Underlying Rationales for each Potential Line of Action/Initiative.
- The last step is to evaluate Outcomes, or Consequences of each Line of Action (see figure 9.1).

This is really more simple than one might think (if people develop confidence in you). It just takes time. It is useful to listen very carefully to everything said to pull off an accurate and thoughtful diagnosis. Listening for side (and snide) comments and watching for body language is vital.

## FIRST, A PLANNING COMMITTEE

Substantial, respected people had to be selected from all K–5th grades. The group had to have representatives from newer teachers recruited. Fortunately, the curriculum specialist came from that school, was active in recruiting them, was trusted and perceived as highly competent, caring, a woman of integrity, committed to the school and staff. She and one teacher from the "contributing" school served.

When about noon I walked into the planning committee near the main office area, people were there and the principal arranged for sandwiches, potato chips, fruit, some candy, and lots of markers. I had lugged in my

24″ × 36″ chart paper, along with tape and markers. People were very friendly, all of us covertly sizing each other up, as we ate and socialized.

## Introductions

We settled down and everyone introduced themselves, some personal stuff, some professional. The principal introduced me, mostly stressing very briefly my work as a teacher and administrator, working with a variety of schools. We had a representative from every grade, the principal, the curriculum assistant, a technology/graphics specialist who took notes, and I.

The graphics expert, who was really talented, was able to transfer my printing on the long, taped-up sheets of chart paper into figures that made my illegible scratchings very legible. She was able to construct graphic figures, a terrific help in visualizing issues, as can be seen in figure 9.1. She did this on the spot, so that minutes were available immediately at the end of each meeting (meeting Barnard's [1938] admonition of establishing direct lines of communication as one of his three indispensable elements of executive function [establishing a common purpose and a system of cooperation are the other two]).

## Purposes

The principal explained purposes, one of which was to deal with the conflict, another to think about moving toward vertical teaming, and anything else we could come up with to improve the school and learning for kids. This was a pretty wide-open agenda, so people knew their input was crucial. We then moved to using the Organizational Mapping model to develop insights.

## DEVELOP EVERYONE'S CONCERNS AND ISSUES

People usually respond to this relatively forthrightly, openly (so I felt they were beginning to trust me). The first Issue/Concern raised was that of *team trust/distrust/rumors*. People felt that distrust was a major issue. The group from the other school was quite taken aback by this perception of them/us, by perceptions of *schisms*. (Not to worry, though, by October of the following semester, this had disappeared from the radar and didn't register as a blip.)

There I was, up on a step stool, marking Issues and Concerns on long sheets of chart paper, all taped together. As figure 9.1 indicates, a number of issues surfaced, which are summarized in the succeeding column, Summarizing Concerns and Issues.

- Team trust/distrust rumors swirling about, creating schisms in the school, generating distrust, them/us feelings
- Team building needed to improve functioning
- Curriculum a concern:
  - in terms of aligning
  - differing views about what curriculum to use
  - some ignoring alignments
- Communication a major concern:
  - communication with administration
  - among teams, within, across, among grade levels
- Bickering, struggles for control, differences of opinion personalized, leading to hurt feelings
- Size of school an important issue in functioning of organizations
- Size of teams, some being eight teachers (to which I responded that that was too large to communicate and to work together. Thelen [1949] noted the maximum number of roles available in workgroups appeared to be seven. Once you had more than seven, quieter, less assertive persons will be squeezed out, participating less).
- In its first three years, the school grew, causing staff mobility
- Faculty felt their autonomy (synonymous with professionalism) was honored
- Social and economic changes occurring in the community:
  - parent participation declining
  - PTA conferences not as well attended
  - fewer chaperones available for field trips
  - more grandparents raising kids
  - more single moms working and raising kids

- An influx of immigrants, some doubling and tripling families living in houses:
  - greater cultural diversity occurring leading to misunderstanding
  - more bilingual needs for students, nineteen languages spoken
  - some kids not motivated

I asked how satisfied people felt with **recognition** they were getting:

- A key person left (the charismatic second-in-command) in the previous midyear, causing great sense of loss, purpose, hurt feelings, morale
- The group from the other school coming on board, leading to little trust, them/us feelings
- Gifted program needs addressing: "It doesn't appear that much has been going on this year."

We impatient Americans might ask: What kinds of *actions* can be taken to deal with the situation?

By now, you, the reader, must feel somewhat overwhelmed, but do not fret. We will immediately deal with that by Summarizing the Concerns and Issues, actually the next section.

## SUMMARIZE CONCERNS AND ISSUES (OR, YOU'LL BE OVERWHELMED)

This may seem complex, since we elicited so many Issues and Concerns. So, it becomes necessary to Summarize them, or we become overloaded with too many details, unable to see the overall picture. Summarizing consolidates Issues and Concerns, helping point out overall patterns.

- Distrust hampers effective team functioning.
- Faculty lacks knowing and applying skills to team properly:
  - team building necessary
  - schisms: faculty apparently not accepting differences among each other—presently.
- Some teams malfunctioning:
  - people do not know how to resolve conflict

- we have to reduce the "them/us" mentality
- size of teams a contributing factor
- Size of school contributing to concerns, distrust, alienation
- Communication with administration, across and among teams and grade levels insufficient, short-circuiting cooperation and coordination
- Community experiencing socioeconomic changes:
  - more immigrants
  - greater cultural diversity arising, creating communications, understanding, acceptance issues
  - community participation declining
- Heightened feelings creating problems with interpreting, *accepting others*, *generating distrust*
- People have strong needs for recognition, acceptance, autonomy
- Conflict over which curriculum to use

## DIG OUT UNDERLYING THEMES (SEE COLUMN 3)

Analyzing for Underlying Themes makes potential for action easier, since fewer Themes exist than Summary items, helps point up the "big picture."

- Trust/mistrust. Trust is essential for an organization to thrive
- Unification and consistency necessary, interpersonal strife causing tension/mistrust
- Teams developing problems, need support to improve, such as team building, conflict resolution exercises: excessive bickering, struggles for control
- Size of teams and school generating problems. Need to decentralize to teams, small learning communities (SLCs) (Sullivan and Glanz 2006)
- Changing community changes student attitudes toward school; parent participation declining
- Multicultural planning needed
- We humans need recognition
- Curriculum needs to develop in a unified direction

Themes also help discern underlying dimensions to achieve action, essential for focusing efforts.

# DEVELOP POTENTIAL LINES
# OF ACTION/INITIATIVES

Now that we've analyzed Issues and Concerns, Summarized them, and uncovered Underlying Themes, we have a flow of analysis. This next flow, developing Potential Lines of Action/Initiatives (potential remedies) in this Analysis of Dynamics of Organizational Change strategy, is based on the preceding analysis of Underlying Themes.

The following comprise Potential Lines of Action or Initiatives:


• Develop trust-building exercises.
• Develop team-building and conflict-resolution exercises.
• Implement exercises to help people understand and accept each other, such as the Gregorc Style Delineator (1982b).
• Open lines of communications; make communication a riveting priority (Barnard 1938).
• Develop Lines of Action to decentralize to teams and SLCs:
  • produces more people included in ownership, recognition, teaming, communication;
  • reduce team size from eight to four;
  • decentralization personalizes, since we deal with fewer people, units are smaller, so we get to know each other better; and
  • reduces conflict.
• Develop major parent involvement effort.
• Establish a Multicultural Planning Committee.
• Develop a major recognition program for everyone.
• Establish a curriculum steering committee.


# UNDERLYING RATIONALE FOR EACH
# POTENTIAL LINE OF ACTION

*Reflective Question*

*Why develop a rationale?*

Dewey (1938) and a host of others note that theory usually underlies successful action, that theory is highly practical. It is necessary to develop a Rationale to support each Potential Line of Action.

- Develop trust
  - The underlying rationale for developing trust is: cooperation rests on trust. If you distrust someone or an organization, you cannot work effectively with that person or organization you feel you must watch carefully (Bryk and Schneider 2002).
- Team building
  - Team building is essential for teams to function more effectively and efficiently, as are conflict resolution techniques. Burying anger and other emotions, which elementary faculties frequently do, impedes constructing healthy relationships and organizational processes. People at first felt this was painful.
- Using a personality style instrument for team building, improving understanding, acceptance, and communication.
  - Implementing a personality style instrument exercise has never failed to help most people become more aware of, accept, and respect themselves, others, parents, students, siblings, administrators, authority figures, virtually everyone. Administering the Gregorc Style Delineator (chapter 3) facilitated faculty to understand and to accept each other. People realized that the other person was not doing something to spite or to challenge them, but that that was their way of reacting as a personality to situations.

## CONSEQUENCES/OUTCOMES

It is clear that the Organizational Mapping process did exactly that.

- It uncovered dynamics the organization was generating so that we could diagnose, analyze, and implement changes to achieve goals.
- Implementing the Gregorc was effective in facilitating considerably improved faculty understanding and acceptance of themselves and of each other. Additionally, styles of each staff member were listed.

- Trust-building exercises helped improve trust—open discussion reduced distrust.
- Team-building exercises fulfilled their goal.
- Relationships among teachers from the other school and those from Southwood had improved so much by the beginning of the fall semester that distrust had completely disappeared. The teacher from that group, who served on the planning committee, said, "All we wanted was to be happy," which struck a chord. That ended the issue.
- Focusing intently on making sure that we communicated discoveries of the Planning Committee to everyone paid off handsomely, since no one possibly could feel left out. Shortly after the end of each meeting, everyone had duplicated minutes in hand. Direct, short lines of communication were established (as Barnard [1938] indicated).
- Decentralization into SLCs and teams moved ahead.
- Team sizes reduced from eight to four.
- The Planning Committee unanimously agreed people were free to choose to team—or not.
- A major parent involvement program developed, including a Multicultural Planning Committee, and a Community Partnership Committee.
- A major recognition program was developed, implemented by a huge "Southwood Bulletin Board" placed in an area with heavy traffic, run by a Recognition Committee.
- A better sense of community among staff was promoted with a "Wonderful Wednesday" monthly program, each sponsored by a different team, who devised clever names for themselves, designing different activities for each session.
- Curriculum structure was devised to generate curriculum *as a routine*.

## ANALYSIS

### More Results

Analyzing the Gregorc provided an outlet for humor as people became more familiar with idiosyncrasies individual personalities generate. People were able to laugh at themselves. For example, asking a strongly concrete sequential person how he or she shops at a grocery store might elicit the response that his/her shopping list is organized by the store's aisles, to which the abstract randoms respond with gales of laughter (they lose their lists—if ever bothering to make them). He/she is a perfectionist, a loner.

*Reflective Question*

*Whenever a party is to be organized, whom do you expect will volunteer?*

Of course the abstract random will love to do it, will have lots of food, loud music, hordes of people. They love to work with others. The concrete sequential? He will not want to come, will come on time, will hide in a corner hating the loud music, will leave first.

*Reflective Question*

*Who will love to fix any equipment?*

The concrete random, who will take it apart to see how it works, but will often bandwagon to another of his many projects, not bother putting it back together again (it's too boring).

The abstract sequential is a reader, thinks deeply, is a great analyst—a loner. We overheard teachers teasing the principal (a very strong abstract sequential personality) with, "I can tell it's your abstract sequential personality kicking in again. I know, you need to think about it, and then we can talk about it tomorrow." Her district superintendent approached every conference with, "Please don't talk to me about what you've been thinking. It just makes my brain hurt."

## Using Barnard's (the Father of Administration) Three Indispensable Elements to All Organizations— To Improve the School (Any Organization)

Barnard (1938) noted there are *three interacting, indispensable elements* to an organization:

- It must have a *common mission or purpose* (otherwise it goes nowhere).
- It must have a *system of cooperation* to facilitate achieving the common mission.
- It must have a *system of communication* to facilitate achieving the common purpose.

The Gregorc helped establish a *system of cooperation*, increasing trust, eliminating suspicion. *Lines of communication* facilitated achieving a *common purpose*. Sending minutes with graphics illustrating these processes after each meeting to *everyone* was helpful. Providing everyone with the same information at the same time with full details allows for clarifying issues by those who did not attend. Without a common frame of reference, attempts to recall specifics of a meeting are usually misquoted, reinterpreted, or misunderstood.

Barnard's three indispensable elements of an organization were met. The underlying rationale for developing a *major parent involvement program* is that it promotes *buy-in* by all involved.

## Using Maslow's Hierarchy of Needs

*Maslow's (1954) hierarchy of needs* stresses the third needs level is *social*. People *need recognition and acceptance* (without it they become unfulfilled, and will begin going after it, sometimes in unacceptable ways).

## Developing a Curriculum Structure

Developing a *curriculum structure* (chapter 6) enables a faculty *to generate curriculum as a routine*, avoiding needing a supreme effort to make one change. If people feel that curriculum can be changed *as a routine*, change can become normal, part of everyday functioning. You've essentially destroyed barriers resisting instituting any change, a rather remarkable outcome.

## SUMMARY

The Analysis of Dynamics of Change process performed its functions admirably. Its Organizational Mapping diagnostic function uncovered key

Issues and Concerns, which were Summarized. It analyzed underlying Themes and pointed out Potential Lines of Action or Initiatives. It facilitated analyzing Rationales to evaluate potential lines of action, and was useful in evaluating the developed action outcomes in terms of these rationales.

The next chapter provides insights into the impact of the constructivist strategy and elements of constructivism on the school three and five years later.

*Reflective Questions*

1. *What is your first impression?*
2. *Do you admire the principal's courage? Note how she involved everyone.*
3. *How do you analyze the change model?*
4. *What additional elements would you add?*
5. *People were willing to confront issues head on, rather than dodging them, as often occurs in many organizations (witness Enron's debacle). Why?*
6. *What role did the principal play?*
7. *What patterns did this organizational mapping change model uncover? What patterns did it miss? How could it be improved?*
8. *Do you like looking for themes underlying issues and concerns? What is the advantage?*
9. *What do you think of moving an entire school toward constructivism? Advantages? Disadvantages?*
10. *Why did no opposition arise?*

## GLOSSARY

**Analysis of Dynamics of Organizational Change**   a bottom-up organizational change strategy focusing on dynamics/processes that gum things up.

**Lewinian change strategy**   unfreezing an organization's practice or structure, moving to a new level, and refreezing the change.

**Potential Lines of Action/Initiatives**   possible remedial courses of action to deal with issues and concerns.

**Rationale**   the underlying reason for choosing a course of action.

**Recognition program**   a program designed to provide recognition for achievement.

## Chapter Ten

# A Constructivist Case Study

## Part 2

Courage leads toward the stars, fear toward death.

—Lucius Seneca, the younger, *Hercules Furens*

Wisdom, compassion, and courage—these are the three universally recognized moral qualities of men.

—Confucius

There's nothing like a nice, longitudinal study to document change in an organization (particularly if it supports what you've done). This does.

We started the constructivist change strategy three years earlier, reported in chapter 9. Dr. Isaacson then repeated the process three years later, using the Analysis of Dynamics of Change strategy, as reported in her dissertation (2004). And Dr. Joseph Brown (2006) studied the school two years later to determine whether the organizational entropy predicted by the Tri-Partite Theory of Organizational Change and Control (chapter 5) was finessed with the internal organizational structures developed for Southwood.

The preceding chapter laid out Concerns and Issues brought to the table by the Planning Committee. The process included Summarizing those issues and concerns, next teasing out Underlying Themes, then developing Potential Lines of Action/Initiatives to deal with Issues and Concerns. The next step was to unearth Rationales for each alternative Line of Action (together with its theoretical base), and last, evaluate resulting Consequences.

Figure 9.1 from chapter 9 is the source for the following. Note the *issues*, unfortunately all too normal for any organization. These included issues of:

- distrust;
- destructive rumors;
- misunderstandings, schisms (them/us);
- fighting over curriculum based on faculty schisms;
- communications problems;
- struggles for control;
- teams too large to manage, causing dissention;
- people's feeling bruised;
- changing community;
- more immigrants with different languages and diverse cultures; and
- inadequate provision for recognition, among others.

Now, let's take a look at figure 10.1, summarizing Issues and Concerns expressed *three years later*. Note that old Issues and Concerns fade, are far fewer—and for the better.

Differences are considerable and deep—some would say spectacular. We are looking at quite a different school:

- Collaboration, never mentioned, is perceived as continuing and essential, often during lunch.
- They want to continue the positive climate and culture.
- They want to continue trust-building—built by spending time together.
- They want to continue efforts to communicate.
- They want to continue relationship building; teachers respect each other—they offer support.
- They want to ensure that new teachers have a strong support system— never mentioned before. They believe it is important for new teachers to develop a constructivist philosophy.
- They want continuous articulation of curriculum.

Each column is fundamentally changed—for the better.

Look at the differences in column 3, Themes, best summarized by Lynne Menard, quoted at the beginning of chapter 9: "Help me, I'm

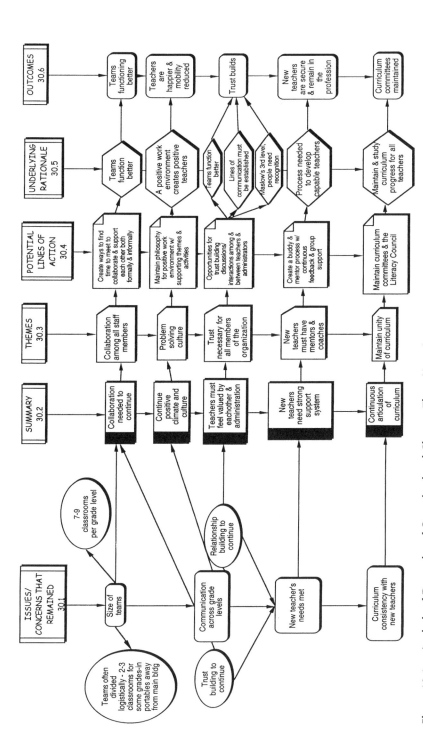

**Figure 10.1.** Analysis of Dynamics of Organizational Change: Three Years Later

drowning." The earlier column is rife with concern about trust/mistrust, interpersonal strife, dysfunctional teams, changing student attitudes toward education, needs for recognition, and parent participation.

## POSITIVE THEMES

Column 3, Themes, in figure 10.1 talks of:

- Collaboration to continue;
- A problem-solving culture being built;
- Trust essential to success;
- Concern that new teachers have mentors and coaches; and
- Maintaining unity of curriculum.

Note what is *not* there—distrust, interpersonal friction and strife, alienation, dysfunctional teams, concern about changing student attitudes toward education, desire for greater parent participation (increased substantially), needs for personal recognition. New concerns focused on professional issues, not egocentric, self-focused needs—far fewer to generate dysfunctions.

### Potential Lines of Action/Initiatives—Very Supportive

Differences in column 4, Potential Lines of Action, reveal fundamental differences. The earlier column wants initiatives to improve trust, and cooperation, team building, using a personality style instrument so people understand and accept each other, develop a process to recognize anyone doing anything significant, develop a Multicultural Planning Committee to deal proactively with incoming people from different cultures, develop a curriculum committee to facilitate everyone working on a similar curriculum.

Let's look at Potential Lines of Action/Initiatives three years later:

- Create ways to find time to meet to collaborate and support each other formally and informally, often at each other's houses. Use **FISH**, the

Gregorc Personality Style Delineator, and "Wonderful Wednesdays" for staff get-togethers.

- Maintain philosophy for positive work environment with supporting themes and activities. Newbies need support, mentoring—and get it.
- Develop opportunities for trust-building discussions among and between teachers and leaders.
- Create a buddy/mentor process with continuous feedback and group support for new teachers, especially in integrating curriculum.
- Maintain curriculum committees and the Literacy Council.
- Establish a clear constructivist philosophy.
- Teams sit in interviews to determine if prospective teachers chosen can fit in and practice constructivist philosophy approaches.
- Teams organize themselves—and the school.
- In addition, teachers want to individualize staff development.
- The faculty wants to cultivate teachers as leaders.

These are:

- collaboration;
- trust building, forming relationship;
- asked for help, received it;
- value of personality styles;
- value of positive attitude; and
- took on leadership roles.

The faculty moved into professional strategies to continue improving. The Literacy Council is new, as is maintaining the philosophy, never mentioned earlier. Collaboration was a dream, supporting each other was never mentioned earlier. Mentoring new teachers was not on the radar, nor was coaching them.

## OUTCOMES THREE YEARS LATER

Let's take a look at the large number of Outcomes, the last column in figure 10.1.

- The organization's dynamics were uncovered, providing opportunity to deal with issues and concerns.
- The personality style instrument improved trust and acceptance.
- Team building exercises worked.
- Relationships among people from different schools improved.
- Communication patterns improved.

## Decentralizing in Small Learning Communities (SLCs)

- Decentralizing into teams and SLCs worked.
- Team sizes reduced.
- Teaming optional, depending on teacher readiness.
- A major parent involvement program initiated.
- A Multicultural Planning Committee started.
- A major recognition program initiated.
- Wonderful Wednesday monthly programs promoted sense of community.
- A curriculum structure was developed to generate curriculum *as a routine*.

The teacher recognition program worked like a charm. Next, the Multicultural Planning Committee sponsored an evening event in which kids and parents (by then over fifty different nationalities and cultures) brought in a small tapestry identifying key items revealing their culture. The faculty expected at most a hundred, and were stunned as over 680 were brought in. These then served as the stage backdrop, covering it from wall to wall.

From a large number of Outcomes earlier, we find a handful three years later in figure 10.1.

- The constructivist strategy worked.
- Teams and small learning communities are functioning better.
- Teachers expressed their happiness directly—teacher mobility evaporated.
- Trust kept building—they worked at it.

- New teachers are more secure, want to stay in teaching.
- Curriculum committees continue work.
- Cultivate teachers as leaders.
- A constructivist philosophy was established, driving the school.

## Development of Key Supportive Internal Structures

- Professional learning/development communities (PLCs) formed, supporting new and veteran faculty.
- Test results on state tests improved significantly.

These are relatively profound professional changes. The school obviously adopted a constructivist philosophy and articulated it. Their focus is on relationships among themselves, since they are a team and small learning community operation, with a variety of team and nongraded models used. And their focus is on improving kids' education.

Isaacson drew several conclusions and implications:

1. Constructivism can be used as an educational organizational change model to reform an entire elementary school and implement a constructivist philosophy and practices.
2. Teachers believe that standardized test scores can increase from teaching constructivistically—test scores supported this (see appendix).
3. In order to make the school resistant to organizational entropy, a maintenance plan is necessary with replanning every two to three years to continue the process. The SLCs and PLCs are essential to this.
4. It is crucial to recognize the importance of teachers' perceptions in creating an organizational culture with constructivist educational practices.
5. The role of the principal is pivotal. The principal must believe in and model constructivism (Isaacson 2004, v).

Isaacson's themes and their indicators are portrayed in the next chapter.

## POSTSCRIPT: A FOLLOW-UP STUDY
## TWO YEARS LATER: SUCCESS!

Two years later, Joseph Brown conducted a follow-up study to determine whether the school was able to continue its constructivist philosophy and educational practices. Brown based his study first on Isaacson's recommendation that the school be studied after two or three years to determine if the constructivist philosophy and educational practices were able to continue.

The second reason for his study was to determine whether the school could build internal structures or mechanisms or replan to retain the constructivist philosophy and practices. The Tri-Partite Theory (chapter 5) maintains that unless such internal replanning structures or actual replanning occurs every two or three years, the program will be lost. That is, the iron forces of entropy will inevitably destroy any plan in a relatively short time unless the organization replans or develops internal structures to maintain the plan.

Brown found that the leadership and faculty of Southwood did, indeed, do exactly that. The faculty decentralized into SLCs and developed PLCs (Dufour and Eaker 1999). In addition, faculty chose as Isaacson's replacement her former assistant principal over fifteen candidates, some of whom had no idea regarding what constructivism looked like. Together, they created a mentoring program for new teachers and others, with pull-out days for new teachers as a mentoring device.

The SLCs and PLCs with the mentoring features essentially function as self-renewing strategies to undo the hovering forces of entropy.

## SUMMARY

Constructivism can be used as an educational organizational change model to reform an entire school and implement a constructivist philosophy and practices. Issues and concerns that dominated the faculty literally disappeared, replaced by concern for supporting each other, for mentoring new teachers to improve their teaching and feelings of support and success. Teachers bought into constructivism strongly and forced the hiring of a principal who supported the philosophy, their levels of satisfaction clearly manifested. Test scores improved significantly.

As a consequence, the school developed a wide reputation in a very large county district as singular, unique—and very good.

## GLOSSARY

**FISH**   a game developed by the Seattle Fish Market to make work more fun, adapted by Southwood.

## Chapter Eleven

# At Last, What Does a Constructivist School Look Like?

When your knowledge changes, the universe changes. We are what we know.

—James Burke, *The Day the Universe Changed*

A good leader inspires others with confidence in him or her; a great leader inspires them with confidence in themselves.

—Author unknown

When I was with you March 8 I learned that a constructivist life makes one's dreams the *pedestal*, not the ceiling.

—Jean Kern, educator, Peace Corps activist

*Reflective Questions*

1. *If you walked into a school touted as constructivist, what **indicators** are keys to recognizing it?*
2. *Next, how can we design a constructivist environment?*
3. *What we're asking is, how can I improve my (and others') professional leadership roles?*

Finally—we synthesize key elements of constructivist leadership. Hopefully, we've pretty well nailed down what constructivism is all about in chapters 1 and 2. Fortunately, some literature has emerged recently concerning constructivist teaching to support the philosophically based educational practices cited, starting with Brooks and Brooks's 1993 pioneer work (although Driver and Easley [1978] studied how students learned science—discovering it's a constructivist process).

However, we're not so lucky with constructivist leadership, administration, and supervision. To this point, only four books plus two dissertations (for both of which I was major professor) have come off the presses on constructivist leadership. Two are by Linda Lambert, et al., *The Constructivist Leader* (1995; 2nd ed., 2002), and *Who Will Save Our Schools? Teachers as Constructivist Leaders* (1996). The other two are by me, *Leadership for Constructivist Schools* (2000b), and *Case Studies in Constructivist Leadership and Teaching* (2003a). Robert Starratt (2002) wrote an insightful article redesigning a supervisory course to a constructivist model and process.

Leanna Isaacson's dissertation (2004) focused on teachers' perceptions of using constructivism as a reform strategy to change her entire large school into one where every teacher used constructivist practices, based on implementing a constructivist philosophy school-wide to provide a foundation for practice. I also served as consultant, describing this process in chapters 9 and 10, and in my second book. In other words, we used constructivist change strategies as an educational reform model for a whole school.

Joseph Brown (2006) just finished a dissertation focused on whether the constructivist school developed by Dr. Isaacson could survive the ravages of organizational **entropy**, which the Tri-Partite Theory of Organizational Succession and Control (Wilson, Byar, Shapiro, and Schell 1969; Shapiro 2000b) predicts will happen unless replanning takes place within two to three years, and/or whether internal organizational structures are established to renew the organization as a routine (see chapter 6 for one model, a Curriculum Steering Committee structure).

Brooks and Brooks (1993) thought that constructivist approaches could only occur in classrooms, not a total school. These, plus a few sources, provide some research-based and empirical ideas about necessary components of leadership and processes to create a constructivist school. So, here we go.

## ORGANIZATION OF THIS CHAPTER

First, we'll skim over the landscape of some major theories, models, and styles of leadership that have been developing for almost a century to provide perspective to constructivist leadership's emergence within the last decade.

Following Isaacson's (2004) conclusions, we'll start with the necessity of developing a constructivist philosophy as the guiding prism by which to focus all actions. This sets us up admirably with a reprise of Barnard's (1938) fundamental insights into the functions of administration and leadership. We consider Lambert's pioneer contributions to constructivist leadership thought, which fit into the analysis of dynamics of organizations (positions, roles, role expectations, social systems, norms, culture) analyzed in chapters 4 and 5.

We'll focus on *relationships* as fundamental to building constructivist leadership, pointing out that decentralizing through developing **small learning communities (SLCs)** and **professional learning communities (PLCs)** are essential to developing and maintaining constructivist organizations and leadership. Developing trust is essential for constructing positive relationships.

We note that constructivist leadership counters our penchant for the increasing size of organizations. After dealing with the newish SLCs movement (whimsically illustrated by Harry Potter's house, Gryffindor), we'll point to the emergence of supportive PLCs, a crucial outcome of developing a constructivist organization, far different than the anonymity and **anomie** large organizations virtually inevitably generate.

Next, we'll explore Isaacson's conclusions and reflections from developing a constructivist school for seven years, which include developing a constructivist philosophy, three dimensions of leadership and six of teachers as leaders, and a final dimension of **affect** in addition to the principal's supportive role. Teachers perceived that creating a constructivist school significantly increased student state test scores. In this process, teachers stated that they felt highly **empowered**.

We conclude noting positive results of decentralizing, that involvement and process are indispensable. Last, we'll review the indispensable value of developing internal structures *to make change a routine* in schools and districts. We mention Dr. Brown's (2006) follow-up study two years after Isaacson's study regarding whether the constructivist philosophy and educational practices could serve as vehicles to escape the destructive forces of organizational entropy as predicted by the Tri-Partite Theory. See chapter 5 for a full discussion.

## LEADERSHIP APPROACHES—VERY, VERY BRIEFLY

Fortunately, covering the length and breadth of theories of leadership is way beyond our scope, as is citing the many definitions of leadership. We'll scan the mountain tops, the major leadership theories, piercing the clouds.

We Westerners have developed a love-hate relationship with the idea and practice of leadership for over three thousand years, at least from Homer's Iliad and Odyssey to now. While books on leadership could fill rooms, formal leadership theories and models start with Frederick Taylor's (1911) scientific management's focus on making worker bees' actions more effective, to the Leader Behavior Description Questionnaire's (LBDQ) dimensions of Initiating Structure and Consideration when perceptions of effective and ineffective aircraft commanders were examined (Hemphill and Coons 1950). As for formulations of the construct of leadership, a contribution was Halpin's team's articulation of eight major approaches, with the team deciding to use leader behavior.

McGregor focused on leadership styles in developing Theory X and Y constructs (1960); Ouchi's Theory Z (1981) added to this focus. Contingency and situational theories started with William Reddin's 3-D (1971), and Hersey and Blanchard's (1982) contributions. Blake and Mouton (1978) developed the Managerial Grid followed by Burns's (1978) transactional and transformational leadership theories.

Next to last in this brief excursion is Greenleaf's servant leadership (1977). Two decades later, the most recent theory/model/style of leadership, constructivist, was pioneered by Linda Lambert, et al. (1995, 1996, 2002), followed by Shapiro (2000, 2003) and Isaacson (2004). Lambert proposed that constructivist leadership essentially enables reciprocal processes and relationships to be created among people to construct common meanings. And now, three decades after the last theories of leadership were published, we're ready to attempt analyzing and synthesizing this theory and practice of constructivist leadership.

*Reflective Question*

*How do we do that? How can we design constructivist environments in schools and in personal informal organizations, such as our family?*

## ESSENTIAL ELEMENTS OF CONSTRUCTIVIST SCHOOLS AND LEADERSHIP

To respond to questions in the title (what does a constructivist school look like, what are its essential elements, what do constructivist leaders do, so how can I pull it off?), as well as the reflective questions above, we might use the same strategy as in chapters 1 and 2, namely analyzing and synthesizing key elements illuminating constructivist leadership.

### Build a Constructivist Philosophy—and Chester Barnard

If teachers have developed a constructivist philosophy (and, of course, if the principal also holds it aloft as a prism to focus all actions), the battle is really half over, because they can adjust practice to match philosophy and beliefs. Noted in chapter 5, this fits squarely into Barnard's (1938) seminal thinking in *The Functions of the Executive*, where he converted questions concerning leadership's purpose into looking at its functions. Barnard formulated three interlocking key functions of leadership.

1. The administrator/leader must facilitate *developing a purpose* to which all the organization can subscribe in their actions.
2. The mechanism for accomplishing that is that the leader must *establish a system of communication*, so that everyone has a direct line of communication.
3. The third major function is to *develop a system of cooperation* to achieve the common purpose.

We cannot achieve a system of cooperation without establishing a system of direct communication for all members. Thus, a key to following Barnard's shrewd insights is to develop a constructivist philosophy. If we generate a constructivist philosophy that virtually everyone believes in and practices, we can begin to develop a common purpose. Big achievement!

### Developing Positive Relationships and Shared Meanings—Linda Lambert, et al.'s Major Contributions

To pull this off, we need to establish positive relationships among folks. This is where Linda Lambert and her coauthors' (1995, 1996, 2002) pioneer contributions to leadership thought fits in. The aptly titled *The Construc-tivist Leader* was followed by *Who Will Save Our Schools? Teachers as Constructivist Leaders* (1996), which points to the teacher as the focus in reforming American schools. Lambert, et al.'s first book emphasized "*Reciprocal relationships*, the meanings of which must be discussed and commonly construed in schools, are the basis through which we make sense of our world, continually define ourselves, and 'coevolve,' or grow together" (1995, 36, emphasis mine).

Lambert defined constructivist leadership as "adults in a community can work together to construct meaning and knowledge" (32). Thus, lead-ership is essentially enabling *reciprocal processes and relationships* to construct common meanings. She cited Poplin and Weeres (1993) in that the most important factor in schools is *relationships*. Isaacson's findings, discussed in full later, support this in spades.

Developing common meanings among people leads to establishing a common subculture (chapter 4). As people interact and develop common meanings, they create shared norms and customs, shared meanings, and shared expectations, which people develop in social living (Linton 1955). We've just described how people create social systems and a culture. Note that we develop patterns of norms by interacting, which coalesce into pat-terns of shared, learned behavior—a culture.

This is exactly what my first book, *Leadership for Constructivist Schools* (2000b), does, that is, digging into the dynamics of schools, such as positions, roles, norms, working with social systems, and deliberately developing the organization's culture. (This comprises the focus of sec-tion III, chapters 4 through 8, since if we do not understand how schools and social systems work, and how to make them work, we're going to be successful only if we're exceedingly lucky, and generally will generate huge problems, [often highly negative] in accomplishing any goals.)

Not surprisingly, section III's ideas fit in admirably as we try to tease out and synthesize key elements of constructivist leadership. Clearly, we are dealing with the structure and processes of organizations, as role ex-pectations become established and roles develop. Role expectations can lead people to be institutionally focused (nomothetic), or highly individu-ally focused (idiographic)—or, a combination of the two. (Thanks to Guba and Getzels [1957] and Getzels and Thelen [1960].) We now have a framework to understand and to predict role conflict.

A major key is how these elements fit together as we create a system of cooperation to achieve a common purpose. As we interact, we develop social systems, that is, any two or more people engaged in meaningful interaction (chapter 4). Grasping relationships of key social systems to each other is absolutely essential in leading organizations. Disaster looms if a person in a leadership position is ignorant of relationships among key social systems.

Another basic theoretical and practical support for Lambert's basic idea that constructivist leadership is created through development of reciprocal relationships that lead to creating shared meanings is the fundamental work of George Herbert Mead's (1934) approach to developing a "self" and analyzing the "act."

Discussed in chapter 3, Mead noted that the self we humans develop is created through interaction with others, which leads us to treat ourselves as an object. Thus, we also interact with ourselves, that is, we frequently carry on an internal communication with ourselves. Not only that, but as we interact with others, we react to our interpretations of their words and behavior. We imagine their intentions, and, hopefully, often are correct because we have developed shared, common meanings.

*Reflective Question*

*Can you work with someone you don't trust?*

## More on Relationships: Trust and Authenticity

For constructivist leadership to prosper, we need relationships based on trust (Bryk and Schneider 2002), which are developed by people increasingly becoming more open to each other. If I disclose myself to you, it becomes safer for you to open up. Jean Hills (1975), a highly reputable Canadian professor who took a year off to become a principal, reflected on his experience and success. He felt that people believed his relationships were authentic. And note how Maslow's (1954) issues of safety described in chapter 2 undergird developing trust. In my classes and organizations, I always try to structure safety (no destructive criticism, respect all opinions, anything said stays in this room [à la Las Vegas]), so people can feel comfortable that they will not be attacked or criticized, or gossiped about.

Bryk and Schneider (2002) studied four hundred Chicago elementary schools for almost a decade, concluding that **relational trust** provides an absolutely crucial role in building effective educational communities. Relational trust is grounded in social respect and personal regard. They found that trust positively impacted schools' academic productivity and that relational trust is more likely to develop in small schools with a stable community—another support for decentralizing, such as by developing small learning communities.

Further support for the necessity of authenticity in relationships is provided by Poplin and Weeres (1993), in "Voices from the Inside" cited by Lambert, who notes "that there is a deep absence of authentic relationships in schools. Often school community members do not feel 'trusted, given responsibility, spoken to honestly and warmly, and treated with dignity and respect.'" Frankly, I find this quite disturbing, destructive of constructivist relationships and leadership.

Lambert, et al. (1995, 1996), together with Blackford (1995), speak to reframing roles and relationships. Blackford notes that constructivist principals shift their roles to ones that are collaborative and inclusive; constructivist leadership provides a milieu in which people can reframe roles through interaction. Senge (1990) was an early advocate of learning organizations, believing that authenticity is key in developing relationships.

## Harry Potter and SLCs: The Benefits of Decentralizing—and School Size

A school should be small enough that students are not redundant.

—Roger G. Barker and Paul V. Gump, *Big School, Small School*

*Reflective Question*

*Here's an odd question: Have you seen any Harry Potter movies?*

Whenever I ask that, people look puzzled and almost immediately can relate to the SLC model, also called a house plan, a small school model, a hall plan, or a school-within-a-school. Harry's school, Hogwarts, was divided into several houses. His house was Gryffindor, another was Slytherin: Note that this model served to organize Hogwarts, particularly its intramurals, awards, and the like (which developed a strong sense of identity), but not academic classes. Suburban Evanston Township High School just north of Chicago was organized into houses in the late 1920s. Still, we haven't experienced a small schools movement until recently (Sullivan and Glanz 2006; Dufour and Eaker 1999).

Stanton Leggett, a premier educational consultant, famously noted that we can develop a good large school, but it is much harder than with small schools. Decentralization becomes a major tool in developing quality schools and organizations. In education decentralization creates structures and situations where it is easier to establish positive relationships with other professionals—and with kids. In a large inner-city high school I'm working with presently, after less than a semester as an SLC, the ninth grade assistant principal reports significant declines in referrals and increases in attendance.

In very large organizations, the spatial distance we literally experience from each other leads to increased **social distance**, which in turn can lead to distrust, and other undesirable results. I've heard comments in larger schools such as "You fourth grade teachers over there . . . ," clearly indicating that fourth grade teachers "over there" are not a part of my group—and are to be watched. Decentralizing has considerable value in improving relationships because we get to know, and, hopefully, trust our colleagues.

The value of small schools can hardly be overstated:

- Do you want to develop a shared purpose, which Barnard says is indispensable? Much easier to pull off in a smaller body, since people can feel that they belong, because we have built essentially a folk culture where people see and communicate face-to-face daily.
- How about cooperation? Flows much easier in small enterprises because we know each other.
- Communication? Much simpler and faster since it often is face-to-face.
- Climate and culture? People feel part of the operation, so social distance is close.

- In small schools, participation in extracurricular activities is three to twenty times greater (Barker and Gump 1964).
- Do you want to avoid developing destructive student subcultures? (Oxley 1989, 28.)

We could go on. Shapiro, Benjamin, and Hunt (1995) pointed out the possibility of developing a strong, shared sense of community, avoiding creation of alienated kids and "outsiders."

How about the nature of authority? Developing **social controls**? Much easier since everyone knows everyone, in contrast to huge schools where one can be anonymous (see Thomas French, *South of Heaven* [1993] for an example). Fortunately, the literature is now expanding with such studies as Feldman, Lopez, and Simon (2006), Overbay (2003), and Hylden (2005), all pointing to the advantages of small size in designing the internal structures of schools, impacting achievement and behavior.

Similarly, developing SLCs is emerging as a genuine movement with mentoring, supporting, and nurturing relationships possible to develop in a small body of people who learn to work together. Interestingly, when we explore Isaacson's study, we will note that moving the entire school into a constructivist model led to developing small PLCs (Dufour and Eaker 1999), in which faculty developed processes to support each other strongly.

When I started working with Dr. Isaacson's school, no one mentioned supporting each other nor, particularly, new teachers. Mentoring new folks became a major priority as they developed their internal supportive culture to help them become more successful and to keep them in education.

## More on Decentralizing and Its Results

When I was hired to decentralize a 1,200 pupil high school in Delaware, we pulled it off with three four-hundred-student halls. I moved to another district, revisited, and was amazed at differences. In the old structure my administrator friends reported that they were firemen, rushing around to put out blazes.

In the new setting, with a hall principal, guidance counselor, and clerk operating as *an administrative team* in each hall, atmospheres were totally different. (Incidentally, this has happened to every building where we decentralized.) It was calm, people were relaxed, the air was professional. Administrators said that they were on top of things before they happened. If a kid was upset, a team member who had a relationship was around to work with him. If something was amiss, usually kids would let faculty know.

Decentralizing also leads to greater participation in decision making and problem solving, honing these skills for faculty, leadership, and kids. In this process, kids learn to take greater responsibility. Indeed, if we want to teach responsibility, people have to be given opportunities to practice responsibility.

Isaacson took risks to develop a constructivist school, actually delegating restructuring to the faculty. That is, she asked them to organize the school according to their values—and, then, actually left the room. Some worked in vertical multigraded teams, others teams in one grade, while a few wanted to work alone.

## Deliberately Creating a Supportive Culture and Climate

Most of us wander through our organizations (including our families) unaware that we actually create the norms, the roles, and the subcultures in the social systems we work in. Some time ago, I examined my own functioning in classes and schools in which I taught and administered and wrote "Creating the Culture of Constructivist Classroom in Public and Private Schools" (1996), later refined in 2000a. In it, I laid out strategies for applying Maslow (1954), Lewin (1952b), Thelen (1949), and others to construct the culture of our classrooms (and, by implication) of schools to become constructivist. It worked swimmingly. Others who try the processes have been able to develop constructivist practices and process in their teaching and leadership, to their considerable satisfaction as R. D. Nordgren noted in analyzing his saga in becoming a constructivist teacher (Shapiro 2003a).

## ISAACSON'S STUDY: TEACHERS' PERCEPTIONS OF THEMES AND INDICATORS UNDERLYING AN ENTIRE SCHOOL BECOMING CONSTRUCTIVIST

Isaacson and I used constructivist leadership change strategies illustrated by the Analysis of Dynamics of Organizational Change (chapters 9 and

10) as a reform tool to generate organizational change to develop constructivist teaching practices in an entire elementary school. Her study focused on teachers' *perceptions* of using constructivism as an educational organizational reform model.

Isaacson's astute analysis of teachers' perceptions of that process and of their constructivist philosophy and practice resulted in five *themes*, parts of the first four being supported in leadership literature. The five themes, each of which has subthemes are: a *constructivist philosophy*, *change*, *leadership*, *teachers as leaders*, and *affect*. Each theme has subthemes or factors and *indicators*. The five themes are *italicized*.

In my view, the themes of *constructivist philosophy*, *leadership*, and *teachers as leaders* comprise fundamental underlying elements essential to pulling off a constructivist organization. In short, the indicators are keys to recognizing a constructivist school in addition to those discussed above (relationships, trust, decentralization to reduce size); see table 11.1.

## ANALYSIS OF THEMES AND INDICATORS

*Reflective Question*

*What did we learn from this pioneering study?*

## Building a Constructivist Philosophy

The first theme obviously is the base for any reform effort. Absent shared belief systems we simply will not get results they achieved. Subthemes under the constructivist philosophy are fascinating. Teachers recognized that they had to understand the concept, that problem solving and decision making were essential underpinnings. Heavy-duty problem solving and reflection run rampant throughout teachers' perceptions. They also indicated the necessity of reflective practice.

*Reflective Questions*

*1. In your experience, do schools provide time for faculty to reflect?*
*2. How about for kids?*

**Table 11.1.  Themes and Indicators Underlying Teachers' Perceptions**

| Code | Theme/Subtopic | Identifying Indicators |
|------|----------------|------------------------|
| **CP** | **Constructivist Philosophy** | Use of the constructivist vision; higher-order thinking; thinking "outside of the box"; a nonprescriptive curriculum |
| CP1 | Understanding the concept | Thinking about thinking; *metacognitive skills*; probing to think on my own; figuring things out; not given an answer, but justify my solution; find the problem; explain; constructing our own knowledge |
| *(Isaacson indicated that overlapping indicators exist among constructivism, problem-solving, and decision-making concepts)* | | |
| CP2 | Problem solving, decision making | Questions, find ways to make it better, principal asked what I want to do, think first, plan, answers not given |
| CP3 | Reflective practice | Discuss what happened, explain why, do it better next time, examine, prerequisite skills, dig deeper, look back, then look forward |
| CP4 | Risk-free environment | Try it out, experiment, if it doesn't work, try again, work it out, think creatively |
| CP5 | Learner-centered | How children learn, think of kids first, observe, listen, watch, provide opportunities, life-long learning, creative approach, kids can explain their thinking |
| **C** | **Change** | Movement, disruption, anticipation of something being different than before |
| C1 | Evolution of curriculum | Understanding—math, integrated units, any subject area changes as learned, finding better ways to instruct, resistance/excitement, adding on/substituting new strategies |
| C2 | Change of models | *Vertical team* concept (multigrading), resistance/excitement, *looping* concept |
| C3 | Change of teams | Disruption when someone leaves/joins teams, teachers choosing to move seen as negative/positive experience |

*(continued)*

**Table 11.1.** (continued)

| Code | Theme/Subtopic | Identifying Indicators |
|---|---|---|
| **L** | **Leadership** | |
| L1 | Support of teachers | Focus on the principal, negative/positive experience<br>Feel supported, provided with ideas, suggestions, help with students and with parents, not threatened by interaction, empowers us, trusts us to make decisions |
| L2 | Feeling appreciated | Spends time making teachers feel appreciated, recognized publicly and in private, complimentary |
| L3 | Provides a professional work environment | Provided materials and supplies because teachers need them, values input into what teachers want, provided time to work with teammates, feel comfortable, feel safe |
| **TL** | **Teachers as Leaders** | Isaacson assumed that all items identified, relating to team building belonged in this category. If someone initiates a group getting together or organizes a group project, a leader is recognized |
| TL1 | Collaboration | Collaboration, getting together as a group, planning together, working together |
| TL2 | Trust-building, forming relationships | I like my team, like working with my pod members, work well together, get along, know value of communication, became a team |
| TL3 | Asked for help, received it | Willing to ask for help, teachers help me |
| TL4 | Value of personality styles | Understand each other, understand myself, easier to work with people, laugh at formerly perceived irritants |
| TL5 | Value of positive attitude | FISH (Seattle Fish Market Model of having fun) helped me, attitude of play, make their day, importance of positive attitude |
| TL6 | Took on leadership roles | Leadership, mentor, committee work/chair |
| **A** | **Affect** | Feeling words: happy, love, excited, family |

*Source:* Leanna Isaacson

Note also the need for a risk-free environment (crucial) and being learner-centered. If principals are unable to establish and model risk-free environments, people will not take risks. We cannot be hypocrites in our professional practice and call for teachers to risk if those in leadership roles avoid them.

## Change

As we identify indicators, we get a sense of the culture encouraged and supported change and risk-taking. Also, responses were honest, since teachers noted that change was disruptive when someone left or joined a team. Note that the *basic instructional unit was the team, not the lone individual*. Why do I say that?

Simple. The pages of educational reform are littered with failures when only one or two people make a major change. That person is virtually certain to suffer lots of slings and arrows (often cheap shots), slung at them by jealous colleagues. Most often they are isolated, and frequently leave. The team is the basic unit for effective change—it protects the individual.

## Leadership—Three Crucial Factors

These themes probably are the most highly significant findings and conclusions, in that each has dimensions that some leadership literature does not seem to dwell upon at length. Anyone wishing to make significant reform of his school or district might spend time reflecting on these strategies and outcomes for incorporation.

The leadership theme has three indicators:

1. supporting teachers;
2. feeling appreciated; and
3. providing a professional work environment.

The first two clearly deal with interpersonal feelings. While the last is more organizationally focused, it still has connotations of meeting interpersonal needs. They speak to a nonthreatening, highly supportive environment, empowering (discussed shortly), support with ideas, suggestions, help with students. Note how feeling appreciated rings with

Maslowian (1954) hierarchical level of esteem needs (spends time making teachers feel appreciated, recognized publicly and privately, being complimentary).

The third indicator exudes the interpersonal dimension (provides materials and supplies because teachers *need* them, *values input into what teachers want*, provides *time* to work with teammates [a sure killer of team effectiveness and efficiency if not provided], *feel comfortable*, *feel safe*).

## Decentralized into SLCs, so Teachers Become Leaders

Similarly, this bursts with interpersonal indicators:

1. collaboration (planning, working together);
2. trust building, forming relationships (I like my team, work well together, know value of communication, become a team);
3. asked for help, received it (willing to ask for help, teachers help me);
4. value of personality styles (understand each other, myself, makes it easier to work well together, laugh at formerly perceived irritants);
5. value of positive attitude (FISH helped me, attitude of play, positive attitude important); and
6. took on leadership roles (leadership, mentor, committee work/chair).

Even subtopics drip with, exude the interpersonal, which are indispensable to becoming a team. Identifying indicators under each subtopic illustrate the above conclusion with such phrases as: I like my team, like working with my pod members, work well together, know value of communication (shades of Barnard), became a team. *Teachers as leaders* also focuses on organizational factors, collaboration, planning together as a group, taking on leadership roles, being a mentor, working on committees as member or chair.

## Teachers' Affect—The Proof of the Pudding

Note the addition of the unanticipated theme of *affect*, with its identifying indicators of such feeling words as happy, love, excited, family. Teachers not only liked being there, they were excited about working there with their peers, even felt that they had constructed their family.

## CONCLUSIONS AND IMPLICATIONS: INVOLVING PEOPLE IN THE PROCESS COUNTS: BUY-IN CRUCIAL

Clearly, one of the most significant conclusions one can make is that the constructivist reform model the teachers and principal constructed met deeply felt needs not usually met in a school, let alone any organization. If we use Maslow's (1954) hierarchy of needs (in order: physiological, safety, social, esteem, and self-actualization), certainly the middle three are not only met, but fully satisfied.

While self-actualization seems rare, we get a sense that some teachers feel they are approaching it. We do not find this level of satisfaction too frequently in most organizations (quite an understatement). Argyris's (1964) later writings indicate that individuals cannot satisfy their needs in organizations.

### Role of Principal Crucial

The principal's role is pivotal since she must believe in and model the constructivist philosophy and practices. Isaacson's commitment to such a philosophy and practice is evidenced in her using a constructivist change strategy (chapters 9 and 10) to move the school into its constructivist model.

Isaacson's implications are fascinating grist for any administrator:

- Constructivism can be used as an educational organizational change model to reform an entire elementary school and implement a constructivist philosophy and practices.
- An underpinning of such a change strategy requires developing and implementing a school-wide constructivist philosophy and practice.
- Teachers believed that standardized test scores can increase from teaching constructivistically. Isaacson's scores bear that out (see appendix, chapter 10).

- To avoid the deadly effects of entropy, a maintenance plan is necessary to continue the process. See below.

## Teachers Felt Empowered

- It is crucial to recognize the importance of teachers' perceptions in creating an organizational culture with constructivist educational practices.
- The importance of affect is critical to success. Teachers must feel appreciated, valued, and recognized—an affect dimension.
- The principal's role is pivotal. The principal must believe in and model constructivism. They are more than managers of things and people. They are managers of thinking.
- In short, a shared, common purpose and a culture was developed, because the principal facilitated constructing shared images and metaphors to construct these shared values, goals, mission.

With the mania to implement so-called world-class testing, and the emphasis on testing every kid to death in the No Child Left Behind Act, the third implication is eye-catching. Teachers believed that they increased test scores by their constructivist teaching and, according to the data, succeeded in their school with fifty-four languages and certainly not mainly middle class.

## AN ORGANIZATIONAL RENEWAL/MAINTENANCE STRUCTURE AND/OR PLAN

*Reflective Question*

*What does an internal organizational renewal or maintenance structure and/or plan look like? What's its purpose?*

The Tri-Partite Theory of Organizational Succession and Control (Wilson, Byar, Shapiro, and Schell 1969; Shapiro 2000b) predicts that organizations lose their purposes relatively rapidly, a process that the physical world calls entropy (chapter 5). How can we beat this process of organizational entropy, where, within a relatively short time, the organization loses its purpose and merely drifts? The key is to develop internal structures and processes that lead to *revitalizing the organization as a routine*. We've described a curriculum structure in chapter 6 developed to pull this exact outcome off. Another model is described in Shapiro (2003a), one that is a single structure. Rules and procedures are provided, as well. The structure has functioned for more than three decades in generating curriculum as a routine.

## Developing Professional Learning Communities (PLCs)

What other internal structures can be designed to keep the organization in a productive phase of its career (either person- or plan-oriented), as was done in Southwood? Brown (2006) points to the SLCs and, especially, the PLCs at Southwood that were vehicles that enhanced and maintained the constructivist model. In addition, replanning is another vehicle, that is, replicating the process that Isaacson did in replanning her school. Developing the internal structures such as the PLCs, or the curriculum structures, or replanning every two or three years is essential to maintain constructivism's philosophic and practice bases—or, the plan and the program inevitably will be lost.

## ADDITIONAL INSIGHTS FROM OTHER LITERATURE, (AND, MAYBE FROM REFLECTING)

### Process Counts

Most of us have learned that content is *the* crucial element. However, in changing any organization from a class to a school, from a hospital to a corporation, process is key. If process is not a major focus, people will not become involved and will not support changes.

Therefore, staff involvement is critical, which numerous studies support (Lewin's [1952b] epochal studies for example). Heavy involvement also avoids top-down decision making common now in establishing state testing and in imposing standards. Involvement is the key to buy-in. Isaacson reported that teachers who left the school to avoid long drives of well over an hour pleaded to return, stating that they could not teach in a non-constructivist environment, nor would they have their own kids taught in a nonconstructivist school. In her school, they felt valued, reporting 100 percent involvement. Buy-in counts. And the road to buy-in lies in the *process* of involvement, which leads to heavy participation, and, thus, ownership.

## Empowerment

Isaacson used focus groups to elicit teacher views. When focus groups ran out of time, all teachers volunteered to return. One of their striking responses—without exception—was that 100 percent stated that they felt *empowered*. With decision making decentralized to the team (teachers and teams reorganized the school, not the principal), teachers felt heavily empowered.

## Constructivist Leadership Abhors Hierarchy

In chapter 4, we noted that organizations tend to generate hierarchical relationships as positions and roles develop. But constructivist leadership flourishes in an environment of partnerships and closer relationships—without status differences. Hierarchies generate spatial and social distance, enemies of constructivist relationships. Constructivist leadership, particularly, values more intimate and supportive partnerships.

To this date, constructivist leadership appears to be the only form of leadership which is not hierarchical. Even servant leadership, although poorly defined (Greenleaf 1977), appears to exist in a hierarchical setting since leaders know directions the organization has to take. Constructivist leadership, in contrast, envisions a shared leadership partnership (note how Isaacson reorganized the school).

Thus, Lambert and colleagues ask in her title in her second book, *Who Can Save Our Schools?* and responds with *Teachers as Constructivist Leaders* (1996). The role of constructivist leadership emerges as more of a model featuring shared colleague/facilitators and change agentry. Years ago, we talked of task and social leadership. Today, it's more complicated. Constructivist leadership can generate emergence of multiple leaders since it actually multiplies leadership to carry out and to achieve purposes established collectively.

Last, the Constructivist Leaders Mental Checklist in chapter 2 provides real insight into strategies and details of establishing a constructivist classroom and leadership practices, as does chapter 6's description of the operation of an internal change structure *which generates change as a routine*, the Curriculum Steering Committee.

## SUMMARY

In this chapter we focused on recognizing what constructivist schools and leadership behavior look like. We noted the paucity of literature, briefly flew over major leadership models and styles ending with constructivism, and dug into how Lambert's establishing reciprocal relationships as the most important factor in schools fit into Barnard's three indispensable functions of the executive. We pointed to the necessity of trust and authenticity in relationships and that the recent development of SLCs, PLCs, and small schools fits into constructivist decentralizing thinking.

We analyzed Isaacson's successful transformation of an entire school into a constructivist model with its underpinning constructivist philosophy, which actually used a constructivist change strategy, called the Analysis of Dynamics of Organizational Change, as its reform model and approach. A constructivist philosophy, change, leadership, teachers as leaders, and affect emerged as major underlying themes and identifying indicators in teachers' perceptions of the processes they experienced. We can use indicators to recognize a constructivist school when we stumble into one.

Implications fascinate as teachers clearly recognized they developed a constructivist philosophy from the process, and increased their students' standardized scores *without focusing on tests*.

Other implications that fairly leaped out were the affect dimension that teachers wanted to and did feel appreciated, valued, and recognized, and the pivotal role of the principal in believing in and modeling constructivism. The few additional studies available recognized the value of process in change, empowerment, and rewards of decentralization. We cited the value of the Constructivist Leaders Mental Checklist as an aid to developing and establishing constructivist teaching and leadership approaches.

We cited Brown's (2006) study, which supported the crucial role of internal change structures, such as the decentralized SLCs and PLCs to beat the destructive impact of organizational entropy. We also pointed to the role of a curriculum structure as another internal change structure to generate change as a routine to keep the organization in a productive phase of its career.

# GLOSSARY

**affect**   feelings.

**anomie**   state of alienation experienced by individual(s) when social structures governing a society collapse.

**empowered**   feeling that one has control over situations.

**entropy**   the process that occurs as organizations lose their purpose and begin to drift.

**indicators**   behavior, customs people develop which identify a theme.

**looping**   schools organized so that teachers follow their kids as they move to the next grade.

**metacognitive**   learners' automatic awareness of their own knowledge and their own cognitive processes.

**professional learning communities (PLCs)**   decentralizing schools so that faculty can develop collegial support groups united in support of each other and committed to student learning.

**relational trust**   people depending upon each other and on a shared vision for success.

**small learning communities (SLCs)**   decentralizing a school into smaller units.

**social controls**   norms and cultural agreements people develop which guide behavior.

**social distance**   the distance people/groups feel from other groups socially; level of acceptance/nonacceptance.

**vertical team**   a team composed of several grades.

# Appendix

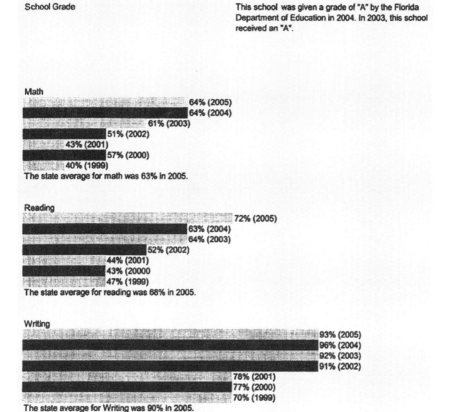

School Grade

This school was given a grade of "A" by the Florida Department of Education in 2004. In 2003, this school received an "A".

**Math**
- 64% (2005)
- 64% (2004)
- 61% (2003)
- 51% (2002)
- 43% (2001)
- 57% (2000)
- 40% (1999)

The state average for math was 63% in 2005.

**Reading**
- 72% (2005)
- 63% (2004)
- 64% (2003)
- 52% (2002)
- 44% (2001)
- 43% (20000
- 47% (1999)

The state average for reading was 68% in 2005.

**Writing**
- 93% (2005)
- 96% (2004)
- 92% (2003)
- 91% (2002)
- 78% (2001)
- 77% (2000)
- 70% (1999)

The state average for Writing was 90% in 2005.

0          50          100

# References and Resources

Argyris, C. 1964. *Integrating the individual and the organization*. New York: Wiley.

Arntz, W., and B. Chase, producers, and M. Vicente, B. Chase, and W. Arntz, directors. 2004. *What the Bleep Do We Know?* [Motion picture]. United States. Twentieth Century Fox Home Entertainment, Inc.

Barker, R. G., and P. V. Gump. 1964. *Big school, small school*. Palo Alto, CA: Stanford University Press.

Barnard, C. I. 1938. *The functions of the executive*. Cambridge, MA: Harvard University Press.

Bausch, K. C. 2001. *The emerging consensus in social systems theory*. New York: KluwerAcademic/Plenum.

Beckhard, R. 1969. *Organization development: Strategies and models*. Reading, MA: Addison-Wesley.

Benjamin, H. 1939. *The sabertooth curriculum*. New York: McGraw-Hill.

Benjamin, W. F. 1989. From the curriculum editor: The test-driven curriculum. *Florida ASCD Journal* 5 (Spring): 2–5.

Benne, K. D., and P. Sheats. 1948. Functional roles of group members. *Journal of Social Issues* 4 (Spring): 242–47.

Berger, P. L., and T. Luckmann. 1966. *The social construction of reality*. Garden City, NY: Doubleday.

Bierstedt, R. W. 1950. An analysis of social power. *American Sociological Review* 15:730–38.

Blackford, S. 1995. *School improvement and a community of leaders*. Hayward, CA: California State University, Hayward, Center for Educational Leadership

Blake, R. R., and J. S. Mouton. 1978. *The new managerial grid*. Houston, TX: Gulf.

Bloom, B. S., ed. 1956. *Handbook of educational objectives: The classification of educational goals: Handbook I: Cognitive domain*. New York: David McKay.

Blumer, H. 1963. Collective behavior. In *Principles of sociology*, ed. A. M. Lee. New York: Barnes and Noble.

Bolman, L. G., and T. E. Deal. 1991. *Reframing organizations: Artistry, choice, and leadership*. San Francisco: Jossey-Bass.

Bracey, G. 2002. *The war against the public schools*. Boston: Allyn and Bacon.

Brantlinger, E. 1995. *Social class in school: Students' perspectives*. Bloomington, IN: Phi Delta Kappa, Center for Evaluation, Development, and Research.

Brooks, M. G., and J. G. Brooks. 1993. *In search of understanding: The case for constructivist classrooms*. Alexandria, VA: Association for Supervision and Curriculum Development (ASCD).

———. 1999. The courage to be constructivist. *Educational Leadership* 57(3): 18–24.

Brown, J. C. 2006. A case study of a school implementing a constructivist philosophy. Doctoral dissertation, University of South Florida, 2004. *Dissertation Abstracts International*.

Bryk, A. S., and B. Schneider. 2002. *Trust in schools: A core resource for school reform*. New York: Russell Sage Foundation.

Burley, W. W., and A. S. Shapiro. 1994. Beliefs, symbols, and realities: A case study of a school in transition. In *Changing American education: Recapturing the past or inventing the future?*, ed. K. M. Borman and N. P. Greenman, 325–50. Albany, NY: State University of New York Press.

Burns, J. M. 1978. *Leadership*. New York: Harper & Row.

Catalanecco, R. 2005. Path to classroom unexpected. *St. Petersburg Times*, FL, August 8, 1.

Damon, W. 1977. *The social world of the child*. San Francisco: Jossey-Bass.

Davis, T. M., and P. H. Murrell. 1993. Turning teaching into learning: The role of student responsibility in the collegiate experience [abstract]. In *Active learning, critical thinking, learning styles, and cooperative learning*. 1993 ASHE-ERIC Higher Education Reports; Report 8.

Deming, W. E. 1982. *Quality, productivity, and competitive position*. Cambridge, MA: Massachusetts Institute of Technology, Center for Advance Engineering Study.

Deutschman, A. 2005. Is your boss a psychopath? *Fast Company* 96 (July): 94.

Dewey, J. 1916. *Democracy and education*. New York: Macmillan.

———. 1938. *Experience and education*. New York: Macmillan.

Driver, R., and B. Bell. 1986. Constructing scientific knowledge in the classroom. *Educational Researcher* 23(7): 11.

Driver, R., and J. Easley. 1978. Pupils and paradigms: A review of literature related to concept development in adolescent science students. *Studies in Science Education* 5:61–84.

Dufour, R., and R. Eaker. 1992. *Creating the new American school: A principal's guide to school improvement.* Bloomington, IN: National Education Service.

———. 1999. *Professional learning communities at work: Best practices for enhancing student achievement.* Bloomington, IN: National Educational Service.

Dunlap, D. M., and P. Goldman. 1991. Rethinking power in schools. *Educational Administration Quarterly* 27(1): 5–29.

Feldman, J., L. Lopez, and K. G. Simon. 2006. *Choosing small: The essential guide to successful high school conversion.* San Francisco: Jossey-Bass.

Fosnot, C. T. 1993. *In search of understanding: The case for constructivist classrooms.* Alexandria, VA: Association for Supervision and Curriculum Development.

———, ed. 1996. *Constructivism: Theory, perspectives, and practice.* New York: Teachers College Press.

French, J. P. R., Jr., and B. H. Raven. 1959. The bases of social power. In *Studies in social power*, ed. D. Cartwright, 150–67. Ann Arbor, MI: Institute for Social Research.

French, T. 1993. *South of heaven: Welcome to high school at the end of the twentieth century.* New York: Doubleday.

Gardner, H. 1983. *Frames of mind: The theory of multiple intelligences.* New York: Basic Books.

Geocaris, C. 1996/1997. Increasing student engagement: A mystery solved. *Educational Leadership* 54(4): 72–75.

Getzels, J. W., and E. G. Guba. 1957. Social behavior and administrative process. *School Review* 65:429.

Getzels, J. W., and H. A. Thelen. 1960. The classroom group as a social system. In *The dynamics of instructional groups: Sociopsychological aspects of teaching and learning*, ed. N. B. Henry. N.S.S.E. Yearbook (vol. 59, pt. 2, 80). Chicago: National Society for the Study of Education.

Glasser, W. 1975. *Reality therapy: A new approach to psychiatry.* New York: Harper & Row.

Goffman, E. 1967. *Interaction ritual: Essays in face-to-face behavior.* Chicago: Aldine.

Goodlad, J. I. 1984. *A place called school.* New York: McGraw-Hill.

Greenleaf, R. 1977. *Servant leadership: A journey in the nature of legitimate power and greatness.* New York: Paulist.

Gregorc, A. 1982a. *An adult guide to style.* Columbia, CT: Gregorc Associates.

———. 1982b. *Gregorc Style Delineator.* Columbia, CT: Gregorc Associates, Inc.

———. 1998/2004. *The "mind styles" model: Theory, principles and practice.* Columbia, CT: Gregorc Associates.

Gregory, T. B., and G. R. Smith. 1987. *High schools as communities: The small school reconsidered*. Bloomington, IN: Phi Delta Kappa Foundation.

Gross, N., W. S. Mason, and A. W. McEachern. 1966. *Explorations in role analysis: Studies of the school superintendency role*. New York: Wiley.

Guba, E., and J. W. Getzels. 1957. Social behavior and the administrative process. *The School Review* 65 (Winter): 423–41.

Halpin, A. W., and D. B. Croft. 1963. Organizational climate of schools. *Administrator's Notebook* XI(7): 1–4.

Hanson, P. G. 1972. What to look for in groups. In *1972 annual for facilitators, trainers, and consultants*, ed. J. W. Pfeiffer and L. D. Goodstein, 21–24. San Diego, CA: University Associates.

Hemphill, J. K., and A. E. Coons. 1950. *Leader Behavior Description Questionnaire*. Columbus, OH: Ohio State University Press.

Hensley, R. 1982. Issues present when entering a system. In *1982 annual for facilitators, trainers, and consultants*, ed. J. W. Pfeiffer and L. D. Goodstein, 140–42. San Diego, CA: University Associates.

Hersey, P., and K. H. Blanchard. 1972. *Management of organizational behavior*. 2nd ed. Englewood Cliffs, NJ: Prentice-Hall.

Hills, J. 1975. Preparation for the principalship: Some recommendations from the field. Midwest Administration Center, University of Chicago. *Administrator's Notebook* 23(9): 1–4.

Hunt, J. J., W. F. Benjamin, and A. Shapiro. 2004. *What Florida teachers say about the FCAT*. Tampa, FL: Ad Hoc.

Hylden, J. 2005. *What's so big about small schools? The case for small schools: And in North Dakota*. Cambridge, MA: Harvard University.

Isaacson, L. S. 2004. Teachers' perceptions of constructivism as an organizational change model: A case study. Doctoral dissertation, University of South Florida, 2004. *Dissertation Abstracts International*.

Kinchloe, J. L. 2005. *Critical constructivism primer*. New York: Peter Lang.

Klusch, B. C. 2001. *The emerging consensus in social systems theory*. New York: Kluwer Academic/Plenum.

Kohlberg, L. 1981. *The philosophy of moral development: Moral stages and idea of justice*. San Francisco: Harper & Row.

Lambert, L., D. Walker, D. P. Zimmerman, J. E. Cooper, M. D. Lambert, M. E. Gardner, and P. J. Ford-Slack, eds. 1995. *The constructivist leader*. New York: Teachers College Press.

Lambert, L., M. Collay, M. E. Dietz, K. Kent, and A. E. Richert. 1996. *Who will save our schools? Teachers as constructivist leaders*. Thousand Oaks, CA: Corwin.

Lambert, L., D. Walker, D. P. Zimmerman, M. D. Lambert, M. E. Gardner, and M. Szabo. 2002. *The constructivist leader*. 2nd ed. New York: Teachers College, Columbia University.

Lammers, J. 1987. Sociology of organizations around the globe: Convergences and divergences. Unpublished paper presented at the Annual Meeting of the American Sociological Association, Chicago.

Levinson, D. 1978. *The seasons of a man's life*. New York: Knopf.

Lewin, K., R. Lippitt, and R. White. 1939. Patterns of aggressive behavior in experimentally created "social climates." *Journal of Social Psychology* 10:271–99.

Lewin, K. 1952a. Group decision and social change. In *Readings in social psychology*, ed. T. M. Newcomb and E. L. Hartley. New York: Holt.

———. 1952b. Group decision and social change. In *Readings in social psychology* (rev. ed.), ed. G. E. Swanson, T. M. Newcomb, and E. L. Hartley. New York: Holt.

Lewis, A. C. 2001. Washington commentary. *Phi Delta Kappan* 82(8).

Linton, R. 1955. *Tree of culture*. New York: Random House.

Luciano, P. R. 1979. The systems view of organizations: Dynamics of organizational change. In *1979 annual for facilitators, trainers, and consultants*, ed. J. W. Pfeiffer and L. D. Goodstein, 140–45. San Diego, CA: University Associates.

Macy, J. 1994–1995. Viewpoints. *Noetic Sciences Bulletin* (Winter): 2.

March, A. 1986. *A note on quality: The views of Deming, Juran, and Crosby*. Boston, MA: Harvard Business School.

Marlowe, B. A., and M. L. Page. 1998. *Creating and sustaining the constructivist classroom*. Thousand Oaks, CA: Corwin.

Maslow, A. H. 1954. *Motivation and personality*. New York: Harper & Row.

Maslow, A. H., and D. Stephens, eds. 2000. *The Maslow business reader*. New York: Wiley and Sons.

McClelland, D. 1961. *The achieving society*. New York: Free Press.

McGregor, D. 1960. *The human side of enterprise*. New York: McGraw-Hill.

Mead, G. H. 1934. *Mind, self, and society: From the standpoint of a social behaviorist*. Chicago: University of Chicago Press.

Mintzberg, H. 1979. *The structuring of organizations*. Englewood Cliffs, NJ: Prentice-Hall.

———. 1994. *The rise and fall of strategic planning: Reconceiving roles for planning, plans, and planners*. New York: Free Press.

Morgan, G. 1997. *Images of organizations*. Thousand Oaks, CA: Sage.

Mowatt, A. M., and A. D. Van Name. 2002. The constructivist leader's mental checklist. In *Case studies in constructivist leadership and teaching*. Lanham, MD: Scarecrow.

Muncey, D. E., and P. J. McQuillan. 1993. Preliminary findings from a five-year study of the Coalition of Essential Schools. *Phi Delta Kappan* (February): 486–89.

Myers, I. B., and M. H. McCaulley. 1985. *Manual: A guide to the development and use of the Myers-Briggs Type Indicator*. Palo Alto, CA: Consulting Psychologists Press.

Nordgren, R. D. 2000. My development as a constructivist teacher. In *Case studies in constructivist leadership and teaching*, ed. A. Shapiro, 40–57. Lanham, MD: Scarecrow.

Oakes, J. 1985. *Keeping track: How schools structure inequality*. New Haven: Yale University Press.

Ouchi, W. G. 1981. *Type Z: How American business can meet the Japanese challenge*. Reading, MA: Addison-Wesley.

Overbay, A. 2003. *School size: A review of literature. Research Watch*. Raleigh, NC: Wake County Public School System.

Owens, R. 1998. *Organizational behavior in education*. 6th ed. Boston: Allyn and Bacon.

Oxley, D. 1989. Smaller is better. *American Educator* 13(1): 28–31, 42–51.

Parsons, T., and E. A. Shills, eds. 1951. *Toward a general theory of action: Theoretical foundations for the social sciences*. Cambridge, MA: Harvard University Press.

Piaget, J. 1954. *The construction of reality in the child*. New York: Basic Books.

Phillips, D. C., ed. 2000. *Constructivism in education: Opinions and second opinions on controversial issues*. Ninety-ninth Yearbook of the National Society for the Study of Education, Part I. Chicago: University of Chicago Press.

Poplin, M., and J. Weeres. 1993. *Voices from the inside*. Claremont, CA: Institute for Education in Transformation of the Claremont Graduate School.

Reddin, W. J. 1971. *Effective management by objectives: The 3-D method of MBO*. New York: McGraw-Hill.

Reed, M., and M. Hughes. 1992. *Rethinking organization: New directions in organization theory and analysis*. Thousand Oaks, CA: Sage.

Selmon, R. L. 1980. *The growth of interpersonal understanding*. New York: Academic Press.

Senge, P. M. 1990. *The fifth discipline: The art and practice of the learning organization*. New York: Doubleday.

Shapiro, A., W. F. Benjamin, and J. J. Hunt. 1995. *Curriculum and schooling: A practitioner's guide*. Palm Springs, CA: ETC.

Shapiro, A. 1996. Creating the culture of constructivist classrooms in public and private schools. In *Global-Local Articulations*. The Society for Applied Anthropology, 1996 Annual Conference, Baltimore, MD.

——. 2000a. Creating the culture of a constructivist classroom and team. *Wingspan* 13(1): 5–7.

——. 2000b. *Leadership for constructivist schools*. Lanham, MD: Scarecrow.

——. 2003a. *Case studies in constructivist leadership and teaching*. Lanham, MD: Scarecrow.

——. 2003b. Designing our structures to do our heavy lifting: What a curriculum structure can do to make our professional lives *a lot* easier. In *Case studies in constructivist leadership and teaching*, 287–304. Lanham, MD: Scarecrow.

——. 2006. Structuring of organizations. In *Encyclopedia of educational leadership and administration*, ed. F. English. Thousand Oaks, CA: Sage.

Sheehy, G. 1976. *Passages: Predictable crises of adult life*. New York: Dutton.

Starratt, R. 2002. *The social construction of instructional supervisors*. National Council of Professors of Educational Administration, 2002 Annual Conference, Burlington, VT.

Steinhoff, C. R. 1965. *Organizational climate in a public school system*. U.S.O.E. Cooperative Research Program, Contract no. OE-4–225, Project no. S-083, Syracuse University, NY.

Sullivan, S., and J. Glanz. 2006. *Building effective learning communities*. Thousand Oaks, CA: Corwin.

Taylor, C. W. 1968. Nearly all students are talented—Let's teach them! *Utah Parent Teacher* (February): 9–10.

Taylor, F. W. 1911. *The principles of scientific management*. New York: Harper & Row.

The Education Alliance, Brown University. 2004. *Breaking ranks II: Strategies for leading high school reform*. Reston, VA: National Association of Secondary School Principals.

Thelen, H. A. 1949. Group dynamics in instruction: The principle of least group size. *School Review* (March): 139–48.

——. 1954. *Dynamics of groups at work*. Chicago, IL: University of Chicago Press.

Trump, J. L. 1959a. *Images of the future: A new approach to the secondary school*. University of Illinois, Urbana, IL: Commission on the Experimental Study of the Utilization of the Staff in the Secondary School.

——. 1959b. *New directions to quality education: The secondary school tomorrow*. Washington, DC: National Association of Secondary School Principals.

Tyler, R. 1949. *Basic principles of curriculum and instruction*. Chicago: University of Chicago Press.

Von Glasersfeld, E. 1998. Why constructivism must be radical. In *Constructivism and education*, ed. M. Larochelle, N. Bednarz, and J. Garrison. Cambridge, UK: Cambridge University Press.

Weber, M. 1946. In *From Max Weber: Essays in sociology*, ed. H. H. Gerth and C. W. Mills, 180–95. New York: Oxford University Press.

Wehlage, G., G. Smith, and P. Lipman. 1992. Restructuring urban schools: The New Futures experience. *American Educational Research Journal* 29(1): 51–93.

Wilson, L. C., T. M. Byar, A. S. Shapiro, and S. H. Schell. 1969. *Sociology of supervision: An approach to comprehensive planning in education*. Boston: Allyn and Bacon.

Your Florida Department of Education. Sept. 13, 2005. http://fcat.fldoe.org/default .asp?action=OneSchoolDetailsanddistrict_number=48anddistrict_n.

# About the Author

Arthur Shapiro (Ph.D. University of Chicago) is a theoretically based practitioner, who is professor of education in the College of Education at the University of South Florida, Tampa, Florida.

His experience covers working in and with public schools in inner city, urban, suburban, and rural settings, plus two nationally famous laboratory schools, one being John Dewey's Laboratory School at the University of Chicago. He has also served on two boards of education, chairing the education committee of one. Dr. Shapiro's teaching is based on a constructivist philosophy and approach, which he models for his students.

Dr. Shapiro's writing and consulting are empirically based on his wide experience and background. For example, he is a pioneer in the small schools and small learning communities (SLC) movement, having published and developed decentralized schools as a director of secondary education, assistant superintendent, and superintendent. He also consults widely in such areas as school organization and management, developing comprehensive system-wide planning models, establishing oneself as a leader, analyzing, planning, and implementing change strategies that work.

He was the lead author of an analysis and recommendations to improve the Republic of Macedonia's radical school reform that decentralized their entire system into independent school districts (all 2500 schools).

Dr. Shapiro served on the Working Committee for Desegregation of the Hillsborough County Schools in Florida as the only outsider, and then he served on the Committee for Instructional Design. He has been and is chair and cochair of numerous dissertation committees (nineteen presently), and serves widely on university, college, and departmental committees. He also received the TIP award for excellence in teaching.

He admires his talented wife, Sue, and two adult children, one of whom, Marc, is a Ph.D. in political science and policy analysis and an international consultant, and Alana, who teaches English literature at Tennessee State University in Nashville.

Unfortunately, he is an unrequited, almost a compulsive punster, much to the chagrin of his decreasing number of friends.